TO OUR PARENTS

who gave us the things
we hope to give our children.

FOREWORD

"He makes grass grow upon the hills."
Psalm 147:8 (RSV)

The simplest thing God does is alive.
It has in it that breath of God,
Life.

He makes the grass to grow . . .
This is a quiet thing,
not rapid or spectacular,
yet who of us
with all our knowledge and skill
could induce growth in one blade of grass?

God's miracles are often small
and commonplace,
but always alive . . .
like a blade of grass.

a blade

DIFFERENT DEVOTIONALS

of grass

Gordon and Gladis DePree have also authored the book

The Gift

DIFFERENT DEVOTIONALS

By

Gladis and Gordon DePree

ZONDERVAN
PUBLISHING HOUSE

OF THE ZONDERVAN CORPORATION | GRAND RAPIDS, MICHIGAN 49506

A BLADE OF GRASS

First printing of paperback
   edition   June 1971
Fourteenth printing   1978
ISBN 0-310-23641-X

Library of Congress Catalog Card Number 65-19504

*"I am a missionary to the Gentiles, and as such
I give all honour to that ministry."*

Romans 11:13 (NEB)

What a variety of things tug at our interest
as we live a year,
a season,
a day.
I want to do this . . .
I really should belong to that . . .
And what about this activity?
Oh, that sounds so interesting!

But in order to maintain any shape in our
lives, we must have some criterion.

What is my work?
What has God given me to do?
What do I call myself?
Does this activity fit me better for it,
or is it a deterrent and a distraction
from my central purpose in life?
What do I want out of life?
What does God want of my life?
I must give all honor to that work.

JAN.

2

*"A man of understanding sets his face toward
wisdom, but the eyes of a fool are on the ends
of the earth."* Proverbs 17:24 (RSV)

. . . if only I were someplace else, I
could do better,
the ends of the earth,
some distant place,
would bring out my hidden qualities . . .
Foolish person!
Wisdom, and the God of Wisdom, are in
your own house!
Set your face to know wisdom within the
frame of your own home,
and it will follow you to the ends of the earth.

JAN.
3

"For he (Isaac) feared to say 'My wife,'
thinking, 'lest the men of the place should kill
me for the sake of Rebekah.'"

Genesis 26:6 (RSV)

Abraham
the man of faith,
was also a man of fear.
His faith
he passed on to his son . . .
mixed with fear.

Fear . . .
Why should we fear the fear itself?
. . . for a man who has no fear
needs no faith!

The fear in us is natural.
We will convey it to our children
whether we wish to or not.
But in this
we must have constant awareness . . .
    . . . that the faith
       we have offered to them
       consciously,
       will be strong enough to cope with
       the fears
       we have passed on to them
       unconsciously.

JAN.
4

"The things that are seen are transient, but
the things that are unseen are eternal."

2 Corinthians 4:18 (RSV)

What is reality?
Is it those solid forms and shapes about us,
or the unseen forces
which guide men's destinies?
We may look about at the tangibles,
and say, "This is all there is of reality."
And a day later,
those tangibles may be removed.
What then would be real?

Only the unseen,
the intangible God,
Only He is Unchanging Reality.

". . . *Worship God.*" Revelation 22:9 (RSV)

What is most valuable to me?
What do I hold to be most irreplaceable?
What would I be lost without?
What do I think of with most intensity
in the long stretches of my thoughts?
What is my incentive for living?
What gives my work meaning and purpose?

This I worship . . .
Is it God?

JAN.
6

"Passing along by the sea of Galilee, he saw
Simon and Andrew the brother of Simon cast-
ing a net in the sea; for they were fishermen.
And Jesus said to them, 'Follow me.'"

Mark 1:16 (RSV)

God's leading . . .
How it puzzles us!
Is it a mystical abstract,
or is it to be found in the natural
flow of human events,
under the hand of God?
Where will I find it?

At work,
Mending my nets by the sea,
Christ will come to me,
and lead me to further service.
If I surround myself with emptiness
and idle waiting,
Who will want to hire an idle fisherman?   —doing nothing

JAN. 7

"That is why I have been prevented all this time from coming to you."

Romans 15:22 (NEB)

These words,
although they contain no specific why in
themselves,
have a great deal to say.

At all times
there is within us a degree of restlessness
to be and to do,
and yet for weeks
or months
or sometimes years
we are prevented from doing and being.
We feel impatient.
We chafe,
and become discouraged.

And yet/ one/ day
God's perfect time arrives;
and we are fit,
we are wiser,
we are ready to do what God wants to have
done,
and He lets us do it.

JAN. 8

"Everything created by God is good, and nothing is to be rejected if it is received with thanksgiving."   1 Timothy 4:4 (RSV)

If everything God created is good, and
God created all that is,
why is there so much evil in the world?
Have the wrong things been used in the
wrong places, and for the wrong purposes?

How can I tell if a thing is good for me,
or if in my particular case it is a
misfit, and therefore evil?

Can I thank God for it, and use it with
good conscience to the building of my
body and soul and mind, as a child of God?
Do I take this thing with thanks,
or apologies?

"... *God himself is judge!*"

Psalm 50:6 (RSV)

There are so many questions
in our lives . . .
so many unsolved problems.

How can those who have never heard
the name of Christ be saved?
If they die in their ignorance,
will they be damned?

And why are men not truly equal,
if they are all created by God?
Why is it right for some to have so
much, and some so little?

And can a confessing Christian
commit great wrongs, and simply be
forgiven, with no eternal consequences?

God Himself is Judge!

" '*I have raised you up for the very purpose*
of showing my power in you, so that my name
may be proclaimed in all the earth.' "

Romans 9:17 (RSV)

To our human ears, these words sound
revolting. We are expected to be humble,
or at least subtle about exalting
ourselves. It sounds crude to come out
and make a statement about one's own
greatness. Why does God do it?

Simply because He is God.
He is no man.
When we invade God's territory and
exalt ourselves, we sin.
We are acting as little gods.
But is it wrong for God to act as God?

JAN.
11

"For I am not ashamed of the gospel: it is the power of God for salvation to every one who has faith. . . . For in it the righteousness of God is revealed through faith for faith."

Romans 1:16, 17 (RSV)

Is unquestioning faith a basic requirement
for our Christian service and witness,
or is it a result,
A thing which comes with practice?
Can we witness,
unconvinced of the supreme power of the
Gospel of Jesus Christ
to right the wrongs of the world?

No.
We will end where be began —
as skeptics.
Only he who begins from faith
can lead others to faith.

JAN.
12

" 'Brethren, I have lived before God in all good conscience up to this day.' "

Acts 23:1 (RSV)

Why was Paul's life so strikingly unusual?
How was it possible for him to be
so daily directed and ordered
by the spirit of God?

Perhaps this could be the reason.
Even though when he looked back
he could see many mistakes,
yet he could always say,
"At this time,
in this place,
I am now doing what I believe God
would have me to do."
His conscience was open before God
at all times.

JAN.
13
". . . the God who answered me in the day of my distress and has been with me wherever I have gone." Genesis 35:3 (RSV)

There are two ways
in which we can be aware
of the presence of God . . .
In those times of crisis,
both past and present,
when there is no one else to whom we can turn,

and in the ordinary days
through a steady sense of His presence
guiding us,
filling us with love,
sorting out our motives,
checking our harshness,
erasing life's mistakes . . .

The special times of distress and deliverance
are our landmarks.
The constant sense is our daily bread.
We cannot eat landmarks,
nor can we set up bread for stones.

JAN.
14
" 'Brother Saul . . . you will be a witness for him to all men of what you have seen and heard.' . . . And I said, 'Lord, they themselves know that in every synagogue I imprisoned and beat those who believed. . .' And he said to me, 'Depart; for I will send you.' " Acts 22:13-21 (RSV)

When God speaks,
it is easy to give a valid reason why
we cannot obey.
God's commands are not very often practical.
They may ask us to do things
which look nonsensical.
They can be rationalized out of the way.

Only a Christian
with the courage of Paul
will hear the second command . . .
Go . . . for I, the Lord, will send you.

JAN.
15

" 'In a short time you think to make me a Christian!'
And Paul said, 'Whether long or short, I would to God that not only you but also all who hear me this day might become such as I am.' "　　　　　Acts 26:28, 29 (RSV)

What is our reaction,
compared with Paul's?
We are in the company of those whose respect
we desire.
As Christians, we speak.
The question is leveled at us,
directly or indirectly,
"What are you trying to do,
make a Christian out of *me*?"
Do we hedge and retreat,
or do we answer calmly,
"I wish to God that you were"?

JAN.
16

"Those others who had given had more than enough, but she, with less than enough, has given all that she had . . ."
　　　　　Mark 12:44 (NEB)

What shall be the measure of my giving?
Would I exchange what I give for what I
have left?

But why should I give at all?
Are not people at best ungrateful,
taking what I offer and expecting more?

And how shall I view giving?
Is my life my own,
or is it a gift from someone?
Something tells me
that when I have given all
except that life,
I am still in debt to God.

Then why keep these things?
Someone has to use them for God,
and as long as you remember that they are His,
that someone might as well be you.
. . . It is only when we forget, that we feel we
must pinch off a piece and offer it to God so
He will not feel left out . . .

14

JAN. 17

"It is not because he lacks anything that he accepts service at men's hands, for he is himself the universal giver of life and breath and all else." Acts 17:25 (NEB)

God does not lack for anything.
Why should I give to Him
my limited means,
my precious time,
my one short life?
Will it make Him, owner of a universe,
any richer?
No.
But it will make me,
creature of God,
more than a dead-end receptacle.
It will make me a live being
through which life flows back to God.

JAN. 18

"Shake yourself from the dust, arise; O captive Jerusalem, loose the bonds from your neck." Isaiah 52:2 (RSV)

As people
and as Christians,
we all experience
the dry dusty moments of defeat . . .
either before the eyes of others
or in the silence of our own hearts.

To think
and dwell
on these defeats
is only to choke in our own dust
to no profit.
We must arise and shake off the dust
and go on,
willing to stretch up our hands
for showers of cleansing
to settle the dust.

But even God's showers cannot cleanse us
while we sit in the dust.
We may,
in fact,
become quite muddy.

15

JAN.
19

"For deliverance is nearer to us now than it was when first we believed."

Romans 13:11 (NEB)

Are we changed into perfect people at
the moment of our belief in Christ?
Any realistic Christian would say no.
I still have the same faults,
the same weaknesses,
basically the same struggles
as those who are not Christian!
It is almost discouraging at times.

Will I never be the person
which the Spirit of God within me
tells me that I should be?
Take courage . . .
We are not perfect, yet . . .
but there is life within us,
and deliverance is nearer
than it was when first we believed!

JAN.
20

"Hezekiah said, 'The word of the Lord which you have spoken is good.' For he thought, 'There will be peace and security in my days.'"

Isaiah 39:8 (RSV)

How mixed are our intentions,
words,
and reasons.
What sounds to be a humble acceptance
of the will of God,
May be a weary resignation to what is,
A hope that things will hold out
until we have left the scene,
an attitude of general laziness.
We don't care,
so may God's will be done.
Surely these words require more of us
than this.

JAN. 21

" 'Have you not heard that I determined it long ago? I planned from days of old what now I bring to pass. . .' " Isaiah 37:26 (RSV)

This statement brings to mind a thousand
questions.
If God determines the way the world will go,
what part have we in its progress
or retardation?
If things will come about anyhow, why should
we plan, or fear to fall behind?
If we will be what we have been chosen to be,
why must we cast about restlessly for God's
choice for us?

A child asked, "Mommy, what will God make me be
when I grow up?"
"Whatever you want to be."
"But I don't know! Then does God still know?"
"Yes."
"But if He knows, and I don't know, will He
make me be that even if I don't want to?"
"I think it's like this. If you change your
mind a thousand times, God knows what you'll
say the thousandth time."

JAN. 22

"Look to the rock from which you were hewn, and to the quarry from which you were digged." Isaiah 51:1 (RSV)

When I look back into the farthest stage of
my origin,
past family,
and country,
and race,
I must think of God,
For God said, "Let us make man in our image."

I think of the qualities and attributes of God,
Forgiveness,
longsuffering,
patience,
kindness,
and looking to the "Rock from which I was hewn"
I see what sort of person
God meant to create me to be.

17

JAN. 23

"They wander about each in his own direction; there is no one to save you."

Isaiah 47:15 (RSV)

Tolerance is a good thing;
we think and work toward
openness of mind,
toward new concepts,
toward new ideas.
But where does it all end?
What is the central point
around which our thinking revolves?
How can we tell if our thoughts are truth?

Jesus Christ, the Son of God,
My Saviour . . .
these words, and their relationship
to the discussion
or theory being considered,
sort out the false from the true.

JAN. 24

". . . Run to win!" 1 Corinthians 9:24 (NEB)

If I am not enthusiastic
about a race,
If I do not set out thinking that
I can win,
I have lost before I start.

If I am not optimistic
about the work God gives me to do,
if I am not full of hope
that in His strength I can do it well,
I might as well quit —
I am already defeated.

But if I enter,
more than
my
name is at stake.
I may not believe that God is within me,
but if I have professed to be a Christian,
and run,
and fail,
Christ is dishonored.

Are you running?
Run to win . . .
This is one game none of us can afford to lose!

18

JAN.
25

"Do not be afraid, but speak and do not be silent; for I am with you, and no man shall attack you to harm you." Acts 18:9, 10 (RSV)

How afraid we are of "attack" if we
speak boldly for Jesus Christ!
Not bodily harm, of course, but an
attack upon our pride, our own opinion
of our good taste . . . or perhaps even
an attack upon the fact that we do not
live as we speak!

But God commands us, "Speak, and do not
be silent, for I am with you . . . ."
This is a command for positive Christian
witness — forcing us to *do* as we *say!*
Silence is negative safety.

JAN.
26

"You do not get what you want, because you do not pray for it. Or, if you do, your requests are not granted because you pray from wrong motives." James 4:2, 3 (NEB)

Why doesn't God give me what I want?
Hasn't He promised to answer our prayers if
we believe in Him?

Have you really asked, or has your prayer
been silent wishful thinking?

And if you have asked,
why have you desired this prayer to be answered?
Was your request offered
with an eye single to God's glory,
or was there another motive,
using God's glory as an excuse to pray for it?

Excitement, enthusiasm, hope
for a request to be answered are good,
when that excitement is grounded in the belief
that this is an opportunity to serve God;
But when the answer is
No,
and I am deeply disappointed,
is it for God
that I wince?

"A man can have only what God gives him."
John 3:27 (NEB)

A serious consideration of this
statement should remove the two most
crippling forces in our lives;
excess pride,
and excess humility.

Am I gifted?
God gave me what I have.
It is not because of my cleverness.

Am I limited?
Do I covet things and abilities
which I do not possess?
Again, if God thought I needed these,
He would have given them to me.

Let these two ropes steady me.

" 'Behold, the Lamb of God . . .' "
John 1:36 (RSV)

The two disciples heard him say this,
and turning from John,
they followed Jesus.

What do I say?
Here I am — a Christian.
Look at me, my life is good.
Live like me.
How dangerous!

I should say,
There He is — God's perfect one.
Look to Him — live His way.
How sure!

Let me watch where,
consciously or unconsciously,
I am pointing.

JAN.
29

" 'He saved others,' they said, 'but he cannot save himself . . .' " Mark 15:31 (NEB)

Christ's nature was two-sided;
the natural
and the supernatural.
He used the Spirit of God within Him
to save His fellow man,
physically and spiritually.
But when it came to His own body,
He suffered the consequences of natural
pain.
If I were indued with supernatural power
today,
how would I use it?
To advance my own interests,
or to heal and touch those around me?

And do I not have the power of God
within me?

JAN.
30

"They were wondering among themselves who would roll away the stone for them. . . . when they looked up and saw that the stone, huge as it was, had been rolled back already."
Mark 16:3, 4 (NEB)

Looking forward to a new opportunity,
or responsibility,
we may be tempted to wonder
if our strength will be enough
to meet the required task.

But how has it always been
for those who put their trust in God?
When we reach that doorway,
looking up,
we find that the stone has been rolled
away already,
by God, to whom it must look very small.

21

"No one can enter the kingdom of God without being born of water and spirit. Flesh can give birth only to flesh; it is the spirit that gives birth to spirit."

John 3:5, 6, (NEB)

A study of other religions
ought not to confuse a Christian,
but to help him understand his own faith.

Some points of Christian doctrine
seem so unreasonable
that we, as supposedly rational beings,
blush to present them as fact, and not as
folklore.
Why is this?
Why do Christian beliefs not seem to fit
into the rational pattern of man's thoughts?

Because they are not man-orientated.
They take a kind of knowing
which does not originate in the mind.
Unless one is born anew by the
Spirit of God,
he cannot see, or comprehend,
the kingdom of God.

*"'. . . pray that you may be spared the test:
the spirit is willing, but the flesh is weak.'"*

Mark 14:38 (NEB)

Shall I pray that no test will be given me?
No,
I pray,
that I may be spared the test.

While I am praying,
temptation to the less than best
is out of the question.
God is in my presence, and I am in His.
Perhaps afterwhile I will be tempted,
but not while I am praying.

So let me pray —
and while I pray, the choice is simple.

really concentrate on God when I'm refusing to be filled w spirit

22

FEB.
2

" 'Be alert, be wakeful. You do not know when the moment comes. . . he has left his house and put his servants in charge, each with his own work to do.' "   Mark 13:33, 34 (NEB)

Constant vigilance,
awareness,
teachability,
freedom from that dreadful state of mind
in which I feel that I have arrived.

I have work,
O God,
Keep me awake.
I would be eager and hungry
for each new day,
satisfied only temporarily by the fall of night,
and resting only to work again,
awake, alive!

FEB.
3

" 'Master . . . I want my sight back.' Jesus said to him, 'Go, your faith has cured you.' "
Mark 10:52 (NEB)

O God,
Have mercy on me!
My sight is so poor,
and my perspective so distorted.

And what do you want Me to do for you?

I want the gift of seeing things
in their proper value,
their correct proportion,
their true perspective.
I want to be able to sense the values
which are eternal, and sort out the
chaff of timewasters.

Do you truly desire this?
Your faith in Me, plus your desire to
have it will give you your sight.
Go. Your faith will cure you.

FEB. 4

" 'No one who does a work of divine power in my name will be able in the same breath to speak evil of me. For he who is not against us is on our side.' " Mark 9:39, 40 (NEB)

Christ's foresight would shock some of His
most sincere followers today.
Here was a man who was not one of their
group.
He was using a different approach.
The disciples were annoyed with him, and
wanted to stop him.

What did Christ ask?
His national background and denominational
affiliation?
He looked at what man had accomplished,
and in whose name it was done,
and knew he was of God.

FEB. 5

"So he ordered the people to sit down on the ground." Mark 8:6 (NEB)

The people were fainting with hunger.
The disciples demanded immediate action
on the part of Jesus.
This was an emergency!

Christ,
slowly, deliberately,
ordered the people to sit down on the
ground,
a commonplace thing.
Was this the way to work a miracle,
in such quietness and waiting?

Am I to say?
Since turning one loaf into thousands
is quite beyond my power,
perhaps my part is to sit down and wait,
if Christ says so.

24

**FEB.
6**

"Then, taking the five loaves and the two fishes, he looked up to heaven, said the blessing, broke the loaves, and gave them to the disciples to distribute."   Mark 6:41 (NEB)

Even Jesus,
the all-powerful Son of God,
did not try to do everything by Himself.
He realized that He could work best
as He drew strength from God,
and cooperated with His fellow workers.

How much longer it would have taken
for Christ to personally give out the
bread to five thousand!
He did not seem to be concerned that His
standing with the Father would be lessened
if the disciples received some of the credit!

**FEB.
7**

"The man who had been possessed begged to go with him. . . . Jesus said to him, 'Go home to your own folk and tell them what the Lord in his mercy has done for you.'"   Mark 5:18 (NEB)

Christianity,
in its purest form,
is intensely practical.

Have you had an encounter with Christ?
Have you witnessed His power
in a given situation?
The first impulse is to sit,
fascinated,
and enshrine that experience,
hang on to the place and the moment.

But Christ says,
"Now go home, and get to work!"
If God has blessed you, tell it!
If God has given to you, use it!

25

FEB. 8 "*. . . but he insisted that they should not make him known.*" Mark 3:12 (NEB)

Jesus knew He was the Son of God.
He knew that He had work to do,
and that He was doing it in good conscience
before God.
He was not looking for titles
or recognition from others.
The secret knowledge of God's approval
was enough.

Help me,
O God,
To realize that what I am inwardly
will be seen,
but an outward cloak of religion
will make me nothing inside.
I know that it is when I feel empty
that I need to hear words of approval.

FEB. 9 "'*If only you will,*' *said the man,* '*you can cleanse me.*'
. . . *Jesus stretched out his hand, touched him, and said,* '*Indeed I will; be clean. . .*'"
Mark 1:40, 41 (NEB)

You,
I,
begging for help with life's frustrations;
O God,
if only You will, You can cleanse me!

And His voice is calm,
almost indignant that we have not asked sooner;
Of course,
I will.
Be clean!

And the thing we fought for months
is lifted as if by magic.
    If we will,
    God will!

26

FEB. 10

"May he strengthen you . . . with ample power to meet whatever comes with fortitude, patience, and joy."

Colossians 1:11 (NEB)

Fortitude, patience . . .
Grim, quiet words,
Straightfaced, determined,
pushing forward sternly.

Endurance, patience . . . with joy!
A flash of lightness
is thrown across the mind.
This is no dull acceptance,
no grim endurance of things,
no mute patience . . .

It is a plastic resiliency,
an elastic quality which snaps back
unbeaten,
smiling,
filled with God's joy.

If we must have patience and endurance,
let it be with joy!

FEB. 11

" 'If you were blind, you would not be guilty, but because you say "We see," your guilt remains.' " John 9:41 (NEB)

If we did not know the source of power
and peace,
If we did not know the one who can bear
every care, and give us ease of mind,
If we did not know Him,
whom to know aright is joy, incentive,
motivation, responsibility,

then our lives would have excuse
to be shapeless,
and tasteless,
and frustrated.

But we have seen,
we have known.
What excuse have we?

FEB. 12

"'. . . Why are you indignant with me for giving health on the Sabbath to the whole of a man's body? Do not judge superficially, but be just in your judgements.'"

John 7:23, 24 (NEB)

The religious leaders were quick
to hold up the Law before Christ,
even to the prevention of good which He wanted
to do.
In the end,
they used the Law of God
for an excuse not to believe in the power
of Christ!

God save us from ignorance
which, posing as righteousness,
defeats its own ends in God's sight,
and in our effective living before others.

FEB. 13

"'I am God . . . I work, and who can hinder it?'"

Isaiah 43:13 (RSV)

The first reaction to this statement
is one of total relaxation.
God works;
what is to be will be.
Why should I concern myself about anything?

But when we consider
how God's work is done,
and by whose hands,
this statement sets us on our toes.

" . . . I am God.
My work will be done by those
who are willing to work.
I will not be hindered by lazy
or inefficient servants,
for My purposes cannot be stopped."

Can the person who owes God much
afford to be indifferent?

FEB.
14
Valentine's Day

"Love is patient; love is kind and envies no one." I Corinthians 13:4 (NEB)

We think of love
as being an active force,
reaching out,
accomplishing . . .
And sometimes it is.

But how often
love must play the passive part!
It must be
the floor mat for busy feet,
the resilient springboard
from which others are propelled
into the world of active doing.

This love
is as quiet and elusive as a fragrance,
but just as surely there.

FEB.
15

"Have you not known? Have you not heard? The Lord is the everlasting God, the Creator of the ends of the earth." Isaiah 40:28 (RSV)

It is comforting to have
God,
Who is as much at home
on one end of the earth as the other.

Where is the end of the earth?
To me, it may be in China or Africa;
To a Chinese or African, it may be New York.
Physically, the world has no end.
But . . .
When I come to the end of myself,
wherever I am in the world,
God is there.
And from that seeming dead end
He can create new life,
and give new strength.
I never need fear that I have not
taken Him along.

29

FEB. 16

" 'I am the Lord your God, who teaches you to profit, who leads you in the way you should go.' "　　　　Isaiah 48:17 (RSV)

". . . I am God,
Who tries to teach you
by the failures of your past,
by pointing out the places where you are weak,
by reminding you of strength you have lost,
that you may profit
and be wiser;
This is My purpose,
not that you may become discouraged
and give up,
but that I may lead you from this day on
in the way that you should go."

Discouragement is safe for yesterday,
but only courage is fit for tomorrow!

FEB. 17

"Through him I received the privilege of a commission in his name to lead to faith and obedience men in all nations."

Romans 1:5 (NEB)

What is a commission
in the name of Jesus Christ?
What duties does it imply?
Do I have such a commission?

It implies that we
in some way,
by some means,
come to know men and women,
come to be such a trusted and integral
part of their lives,
that by the total witness
of our lives and speech
we may lead them to faith in Jesus Christ
and obedience to the Holy Spirit.

Can any Christian be uncommissioned?

FEB.
18

"We knelt down on the beach and prayed, then bade each other good-bye."

Acts 21:5 (NEB)

In the New Testament,
we find no shyness among Christians
toward being what they were,
Christians.

Why are we more hesitant?
For them, Christianity was the new,
the exciting,
the bold,
the sometimes forbidden and dangerous.

Is our faith so old,
so safe, so accepted,
that we look upon public acknowledgement
and open witness,
as overstatement of an obvious fact?

If this is our attitude,
Someday the fact of Christianity
may not be so obvious.

FEB.
19

"Adapt yourselves no longer to the pattern of this present world, but let your minds be re-made, and your whole nature thus trans-formed."

Romans 12:2 (NEB)

What is the difference
between being "odd,"
and being a respected individual in the world,
Christian or not?

The simply odd person breaks the pattern
because he is ignorant,
because he does not know.
He does not know the rules,
nor the fact that he is being obnoxious.
He only feels the rebuff,
and blames it on his faithfulness,
and his faith.

The individual
is one who is aware of the situation.
He knows the world's way,
but he also knows God's way.
He has chosen,
knowing the world's rules,
and why he must break them,
and what will be the result.

FEB.
20

"To him who smote the first-born of Egypt,
for his steadfast love endures forever."

Psalm 136:10 (RSV)

The above statement
seems to present
an irreconcilable paradox.
How could a God kill,
Whose love endures forever?

Like all of God's doings,
this must be taken in context.
We cannot take a piece of our lives,
and isolate it from the whole.
This only leads us to brood
on God's injustice.
For the good of the whole human race,
and the future of mankind,   *strike is hard blow*
God had to smite in love!
For our good,
known or unknown,
must He sometimes smite us?
His steadfast love endures forever.

FEB.
21

"If anyone obeys my teaching he shall never
know what it is to die."   John 8:51 (NEB)

What do we know of death?
Only the fear of it
for ourselves,
our helplessness to thwart it
for others,
the seeming finality of its robbery
of those we cherish and want to keep . . .

There is One who knows more of death.
Jesus Christ has died,
and lives.
All that we can fear about death,
He overcame.
All that we do fear about death
we can overcome
through faith in Him.

32

"My aim is not my own will, but the will of him who sent me."   John 5:30 (NEB)

Each one of us
is sent of God . . .
sent into our surroundings,
circumstances,
work,
temptations and problems.
To be left to wander in them alone
would be disaster.

But far from wandering alone,
aimlessly,
we are to have an aim,
a direction,
a frame through which to view
and clarify
life's occurrences.
The clarifying process is a simple test.

Does this fit into the picture—
God has showed me
to be His best for me?

". . . that our God may count you worthy of his calling, and mightily bring to fulfilment every good purpose and every act inspired by faith."   2 Thessalonians 1:11 (NEB)

Good purposes,
good acts,
how often they are conceived in our hearts
by the inspiration of the Holy Spirit,
yet,
sadly,
how often they are stillborn
or short-lived!

To perceive the prompting of God
in the heart,
and to follow it through
until it is "mightily brought to fulfilment"
. . . is this not the essence of victory
in Christian living?

"... everywhere your faith in God has reached men's ears." 1 Thessalonians 1:9 (NEB)

People are sure
to form an impression of us,
bound to hear something of us as a part
of a family,
a community,
a society.
What will they hear,
and what will be the gist
of the conversation
when our names are mentioned?

Will it be what we have?
What we do?
What we are?
Will the dominant characteristics of our
lives
be consistent with our Christian faith?

"They ... found they could not haul the net aboard, there were so many fish in it."
John 21:6 (NEB)

I sometimes
find myself with an empty net,
going hungry,
not because the sea of God's goodness
contains no fish,
but because I do not know
how or when to catch it.

There are times when I use the net
clumsily, and fail.
There are times when I sit, discouraged,
in the boat,
and let the bounty swim by . . .

O God,
help me to know,
and to understand how to avail my life
of Your goodness,
and to appropriate what my spirit needs.

*"This is my commandment: love one another,
as I have loved you."*   John 15:12 (NEB)

Can love be commanded?
Is not love
a thing which must grow out of the atmosphere,
an elusive thing
which either simply does or does not exist?

True,
the effect,
the end reward of love,
must be spontaneous.
But the building of love
can be as meticulously planned
as an architect plans the building of a house.
If each piece is laid with care
and thought,
and prayer,
can the whole be anything but beautiful?

*" 'Lazarus is dead. I am glad not to have been
there; it will be for your good and for the
good of your faith.' "*   John 11:15 (NEB)

Afterward
the end of the story always seems obvious.

But can you imagine,
in the disciples' place,
why Christ would wait,
deliberately,
and then go to see his friend —
dead?

We are reading the story of our lives
from the front
to the back,
and there is no chance to peek
at the last page.
But God is the author,
and you can be sure that the answers
will be obvious when the story is complete.

"For the spirit that God gave us is no craven spirit, but one to inspire strength, love, and self-discipline."   2 Timothy 1:7 (NEB)

Am I afraid?
This is not the Spirit of God
living in me,
but the spirit of myself,
crowding God out.

God's Spirit
brings strength,
brings a love for every person I meet,
a driving, disciplined energy
within my life.
Fear — weakness — disinterest   in   people —
lack of self-control . . .
These are self.
The Spirit of God is the antidote.

MAR.
1

"Hoard a wealth of noble actions by doing good. . . . Thus they will grasp the life which is life indeed."

1 Timothy 6:18, 19 (NEB)

It is easy
to construct a hollow shell of a life,
piled with the things
which we are sure we need,
rushed with activities which seem essential,
and inside this shell
to live in a perfect vacuum.

Is there not a point
at which we could begin,
a point of central focus within us
from which we could begin to build,
and let life grow out
from within?
It would not appear to be as much,
but certainly it could not be as hollow.

MAR.
2

"There is one God, and also one mediator between God and men, Christ Jesus . . ."

1 Timothy 2:5 (NEB)

People in all parts of the world
agree that there is a God.
This does not seem to cause any question.

But a problem does arise
when we begin to discuss
how that God must be approached.

There are many answers.
Is it not more tactful to be open-minded,
to agree that everyone has a right
to believe as he wishes?

There are many answers,
true.
But if our sense of Christian urgency
would remain alive,
there can be only one answer for us . . .
Jesus Christ.
By any other answer
we may call ourselves religious
but not Christian.

MAR.
3

"The hour of favor has now come; now; I say, has the day of deliverance dawned."
2 Corinthians 6:2 (NEB)

Just a minute . . .
Oh . . . I must do that tomorrow . . .
When I find time . . .

How common these are in our vocabulary!
By nature,
we procrastinate.
How much easier it seems
to do things five minutes from now,
or tomorrow
than
Now.
Do we forget that when tomorrow comes
it too will be a
now?

In the realm of the spiritual
particularly,
we procrastinate.
We will read the Bible tomorrow.
We will pray about it later.
We will witness when the occasion is right . . .

Now
is the time to be a true Christian!

MAR.
4

" 'Peace is my parting gift to you, my own peace, such as the world cannot give. Set your troubled hearts at rest, and banish your fears.' "
John 14:27 (NEB)

That inner calm,
that peace without a visible reason,
that state of being
which knows not destructive fear
or anxiety,
that peace which is present
as a surprise
when there is every reason to be upset . . .

These are Christ's gifts to us.
Have I claimed mine?

**MAR.
5**
*". . . your faith has shown itself in action, your
love in labour, and your hope of our Lord
Jesus Christ in fortitude."*
1 Thessalonians 1:3 (NEB)

Faith,
Hope,
Love . . .
The three great Christian virtues.

But while they are the eternal values
of the Christian,
they are also the unseen qualities,
the intangible qualities which can only be
given form in the more concrete shape of
action,
labor,
fortitude. — power to withstand pain

These words do not have the fine ring
of faith, hope and love,
but they certainly bear more weight
in the world of men.

**MAR.
6**
*"Behold, in the day of your fast you seek your
own pleasure. . . . Fasting like yours this day
will not make your voice to be heard on high."*
Isaiah 58:3, 4 (RSV)

How many of the good things we do
are hollow!

Others may look at us and say,
"How you sacrifice!
how much faith you must have!
how well you pray!
how humble you are!"

When we know inwardly
that we are often proud,
or frightened,
and pray with emptiness,
and exercise little real faith beyond
what we can see or guess,
and, like the rest of the human race,
tend to follow that which will save
our own skin.

My family
need to care
more, more
humble

Is it the good appearance which is wrong?
No, but the appearance should have backing.

MAR. 7

"To their zeal for God I can testify; but it is an ill-informed zeal. For they ignore God's way of righteousness and try to set up their own . . . Christ ends the law, and brings righteousness for everyone who has faith."

Romans 10:2-4 (NEB)

Jesus Christ
came to do away with all the minute
keepings of the Law.
He came to tell men that after they believed,
they were to live in the spirit
of that belief,
and not to be confined,
and blinded,
by senseless lawkeeping.

Was not Christ afraid that something
so free and flexible as a spiritual faith
in God
would lose its power, and fade away?
Or did He know that it is dictatorships
which always end in ruin?

MAR. 8

"They warned them that to enter the kingdom of God we must pass through many hardships."

Acts 14:22 (NEB)

All people have hardships.
How,
in what way,
are a Christian's hardships of a different
nature?

The bearing of them is different, yes.
But the hardships themselves,
how are they different?

Our standards are higher, and harder to
live up to;
we fight for things we cannot see, and
search for things we cannot lay our hands on.

To enter the place in our existence
where God can truly be called King of our lives,
we must pass through much difficult territory.

40

MAR.
9

"But . . . Paul, filled with the Holy Spirit, looked him in the face and said, 'You utter imposter and charlatan! You son of the devil and enemy of all goodness, will you never stop falsifying the straight ways of the lord?'"
Acts 13:9, 10 (NEB)

As Christians,
we are concerned with conveying the distinguishing
characteristic of our faith —
love.

But faced with the love of God,
and temptation to condone obvious evil
in the name of love,
we are left no choice.
When obedience to God
demands that we speak a positive "no,"
to do so is love.
To do less is to be an enemy of God's love.

MAR.
10

"He followed him out, with no idea that the angel's intervention was real. . . . Then Peter came to himself. 'Now I know it is true . . .'"
Acts 12:9-11 (NEB)

Passing through the hours of the day
and the night,
the things which happen to us
do not seem to be the workings of God
in our lives.
God's acts seem very distant and removed
from the scurry in which we find ourselves
involved . . .

And then there comes a moment
when we come to ourselves —
a moment of realization.
"These are God's acts in the here and now —
    these are God's ways,
    and I had no idea . . ."

41

MAR. 11　"*At that time men began to call upon the name of the Lord.*"

Genesis 4:26 (RSV)

Worship of God
is nothing new.
The beginning of history
records the names of men
who called upon God.

But from that time
until now
is a long way.
I cannot expect to use their tools,
or think their thoughts
or wear their garments.
Likewise,
I cannot echo their words
to call upon God.

God is changeless
and the worship of His Name forever sacred.
But that worship must arise anew
each day
born of my need for God
in the day in which I live,
or it becomes a dusty and broken relic . . .
interesting,
but fit only to be put in a glass case
and looked upon as an oddity.

MAR. 12　". . . *but we, who belong to daylight, must keep sober, armed with faith and love for breastplate . . .*"　1 Thessalonians 5:8 (NEB)

The most formidable weapons
are not always the best insurance.
　Anger brings more anger.
　Blows call for blows.
　Possessiveness fosters possessiveness . . .

But we,
armed with faith in God
will find Him faithful to us,
and armed with genuine love for people,
will find that they love us.
. . . and what better protection could we have
than the faithfulness of God
and the love of man?

42

MAR. 13 *"Stand firm, then, brothers, and hold fast to the traditions which you have learned from us . . ."* 2 Thessalonians 2:15 (NEB)

All the world,
and especially the young,
is grasping for some stable
and unchanging thing.

Progress must come,
and we will only be blind and irrelevant
if we do not think so . . .
    and yet as the mind of man
    reaches out into the world of the
    unknown,
    the heart of man must be anchored
    in a sureness.

I have faith in God.
May the firmness of this faith
give security not only to me,
but to those who will look to me today
for some sense of sureness.

MAR. 14 *"All will hate you for your allegiance to me."* Mark 13:13 (NEB)

We do not like a negative approach
to Christianity.
We prefer to make our faith and our friends
compatible.
We do not wish to have
holier-than-thou opinions of ourselves.

But when, in a group, there comes that
feeling of un-fittingness, of total
un-belonging, of a different outlook, and
dissimilar values,
must we mold ourselves until we are the perfect
form of what the group demands, at the risk of
our Christian convictions?

If there is ever a true and honest choice
in the judgment hall of my conscience,
may I not hesitate to be spat upon
for the name of Jesus Christ.

43

"Try hard to show yourself worthy of God's approval, as a labourer who need not be ashamed, driving a straight furrow, in your proclamation of the truth."

2 Timothy 2:15 (NEB)

A furrow,
the work of a plowman,
is never a charted thing.
He must dig the plow point in, keep walking,
and move straight ahead.
There is no line to follow — he leaves the
line behind him as he goes,
the brown earth turned up, ready to receive
the seed.

Can I drive a straight furrow,
uncharted,
step at a time, with my eyes fixed on the goal
ahead?
If so, then I can be a laborer who needs not
be ashamed of his work before God.

"We are not among those who shrink back and are lost; we have the faith to make life our own." Hebrews 10:39 (NEB)

When we run into obstacles
in our personality
or our environment,
it is easy to withdraw,
to shrink back,
to retreat into a safe state of nothingness.

But as Christians,
we cannot be among those who shrink back.
The only legitimate direction for us to go
is on and up and on.

But today, in this case, with this problem,
how can we?

Is not this problem part of life?
We have the faith to make life our own.

*"We ought to see how each of us may best
arouse others to love and active goodness."*
Hebrews 10:24 (NEB)

We frequently
arouse each other
to annoyance,
to anger,
to jealousy,
to fear . . .
This seems to come without trying.

But as a Christian,
in my family life,
in my church life,
How can I inspire others to love,
to showing that love of God
through active doing?
How can I inspire good ideas . . . in others?
How can I arouse
or stir up good?

This takes a bit more thought.
It also
takes more
than being neutral.

*"Whoever wants to be great must be your
servant, and whoever would be first, must be
the willing slave of all — like the Son of Man."*
Matthew 20:27 (NEB)

It is jokingly said,
"Blessed are they who go around in circles,
for they shall be called big wheels."

Any position on earth,
or in the kingdom of heaven,
which sounds interesting and exciting,
takes a great deal of work
and self-sacrifice.

If Christ is "The Door,"
we must be willing to be the door mat.

"... *pay all the more heed to what we have been told, for fear of drifting from our course.*" Hebrews 2:1 (NEB)

From morning until night
I am busy.
Surely all this motion
is getting me somewhere,
isn't it?

Somewhere . . .
What an indefinite term!
Where am I going?
Am I any closer to being there
than I was yesterday?
I don't know . . .
I've been so busy going,
I haven't thought about
where . . .
Of course, I know.
I want to know God,
Now . . .
as He is revealed in Jesus Christ.
Let's check and see if I'm going
ahead,
or backward,
or nowhere . . .

"*When I am afraid, I put my trust in thee.*"
Psalm 56:3 (RSV)

The Christian's grimmest tests can be changed
into the Christian's greatest triumphs . . .
How can this be?

When I am not afraid,
I can do a thing alone.
And that is exactly where I find myself,
alone.

But when I feel afraid,
insufficient,
fearful of the task ahead,
I seek the God I trust,
and the company is wonderful!

MAR.
21
*"Peter replied, 'Everyone else may fall away
on your account, but I never will.'"*
Matthew 26:33 (NEB)

Peter was so sure of his loyalty to Christ
that he threw caution to the winds.
He had the same attitude that we sometimes
see in ourselves . . .
Evil can't touch me —
I'm a Christian!
The moment our faith
becomes the Peter type,
loud and showy in its sureness,
we are likely to come to our senses
with the cock crowing three times.

MAR.
22
*"You have shown yourself trustworthy in a
very small matter and you shall have charge
of ten cities.'"*
Luke 19:17 (NEB)

These little things!
The world is so full of important doings,
and my work seems so small . . .
How can it ever be useful?
All this small talk . . .
All these small matters to attend to . . .
All these small questions to answer . . .

How will I ever get around to doing
anything really important?
Or will I?

But those small things . . .
Something tells me that they are not to be
despised.
If I am not faithful in these little things,
there may be no faithfulness left for me.
Perhaps my whole life will be small.
And if
someday,
God looks around for one to do a bigger task
will He not look to see
who has done small things well?

47

MAR. 23

" 'We have a law; and by that law he ought to die, because he has claimed to be the Son of God.' " John 19:7 (NEB)

By what law do I judge my fellow man?
When I give authority to my accusations,
am I honest?
When I easily say that a man has offended
God,
can it be that he has only transgressed
upon my concept of what pleases God?

If I would take my brother's case before
God,
perhaps He would not be aware that He had
been offended at all.

Let my doubtful judgments be directed
toward myself,
and let not my judgments of others be
tinged with doubtful divine opinion.

MAR. 24

"Let us therefore cleanse ourselves from all that can defile flesh or spirit, and in the fear of God complete our consecration." 2 Corinthians 7:1 (NEB)

It is difficult to set one's own rules of
conduct, once the conventional do's and
don'ts are questioned.
How can I judge what
for me
personally
is right or wrong?

It is an unseen boundary,
yet the bearer of the responsibility
is the only one who can have the sensitivity
to know.
Does this defile my flesh or spirit in
the eyes of God as I understand Him?
Nothing is worth this price.

Physical
relationship

48

"We never cease to be confident."
2 Corinthians 5:6 (NEB)

Every day
our hopes are high for life,
yet many nights
when we take personal inventory
we know that we have failed.
Our energies have often been spent
on those things which are worthless or
harmful, and the best has been
neglected . . .
It is enough for despair!

But as Christians,
full of God's power,
(used or unused)
we can afford to be optimists.
His power is in us —
perhaps tomorrow *will* be better!

*"Love in all sincerity, loathing evil and
clinging to the good."* Romans 12:9 (NEB)

Good . . .
so many different things
are good to different people.
How would I define "Good"?
Is good not that which is pleasing
in the sight of God,
that which will make the best of me
as a Christian?

Having decided this, however,
is only the beginning.
That small, elusive good which I know, or
believe to be right,
is like a fragile piece of driftwood
in a huge sea of evil . . .
so small by comparison, I may be tempted
to think it not worth my while.
But if I will reach out to catch it,
and hold to it tightly,
I find it able to keep me from sinking
beneath the waters of evil.

Can I afford to turn loose of this small thing?
Like a man adrift in the middle of the ocean!

49

MAR. 27

"For they did not as yet know the scripture that he must rise from the dead."

John 20:9

The resurrection week
which we now celebrate with joy
must have been a horrible nightmare
to the disciples.
They did not know,
they did not understand.
How could they have dreamed
that their most terrible defeat
would turn out to be Christ's greatest
triumph?

May we think of this when we
do not know,
and cannot understand.

Wheaton Taylor

MAR. 28

"God has shown himself a sure defense."

Psalm 48:3 (RSV)

Life for most of us is pleasant.
What battles do we have as Christians?

The battle against pleasantness itself!
To avoid sinking into unproductive
complacency,
one must continually battle.
Mental,
Physical,
Spiritual alertness and awareness
are a continual struggle.
. . . and the struggle is such a sly one,
for it is the struggle against nothing,
and nothing,
the pleasant state of nothing,
is the death of us!

But God has shown Himself to be our sure
defense against all that will harm us . . .
even our own laziness!

**MAR.
29**
"God is in the midst of her, she shall not be moved." Psalm 46:5 (RSV)

What is a sign of God's presence
within a group,
an organization,
a movement,
or even a person?

Calm,
serene,
deeply quiet confidence,
the kind of faith that cannot be moved.
Not,
God forbid,
that which is stagnant and will not move,
but that which cannot be shaken
because its basis is deep and true.

**MAR.
30**
"But they insisted on their demand, shouting that Jesus should be crucified. Their shouts prevailed." Luke 23:23 (NEB)

The voice of God
is a still small voice,
while the voice of the crowd
is a loud large voice . . .

How easy it is to let the still
voice of God
be out-shouted!

Pilate had good intentions.
He did all he could to please everyone . . .
Jesus and the crowd.
But when there came a choice, and only one
voice could be heard,
the voice of the mob prevailed.

Is it possible
to have that still, far-away voice of God
win out over the loud cries heard by our ears?
That depends
where our attention
is focused.

MAR.
31

"Say to my soul, 'I am your deliverance!'"
Psalm 35:3 (RSV)

There is a high plane of experience,
a buoyant,
radiant,
free-of-soul way of life which does not
depend on circumstances,
but comes from within . . .
Yet frequently I am bound about
with an invisible film of self
which separates me from this high way.
My feet are bound,
and I cannot step up onto it,
simple and near as it looks to be!

O God,
say to my soul,
    "I am your deliverer!"

APR.
1

*"Rejoice in the Lord, O you righteous! Praise
befits the upright."*   Psalm 33:1 (RSV)

By what I say
I can create or destroy an atmosphere
for those around me.
As a Christian,
what type of conversation
is becoming to me?

The honorable,
the pure,
the gentle,
the lovely,
the outpouring of the thankful heart.

It is so easy to make conversation
out of the little bitternesses of life,
but so much better
to make much of God's goodness.

APR.
2

"Joy comes with the morning."

Psalm 30:5 (RSV)

As surely as the dawn
conquers the darkness of night,
as quietly and unobtrusively
as comes the daybreak,
So sure,
so quiet
is the joy that can be ours,
fresh and new every morning!

Perhaps they are
the same old words we read,
the same old prayer we pray.
But the joy is new,
like an old sun shining on an old world
to make a day which has never been.

APR.
3

*". . . accept one another as Christ accepted
us . . ."*

Romans 15:7 (NEB)

Two Christians
standing in a corner
gravely shaking their heads
over another Christian's interpretation
of faith in Jesus Christ . . .
This is the ulcer in the stomach
of the Christian Church.

What standard shall we set
for the genuine Christian?
Behavior patterns are hopeless . . .
they lead to nothing but dissension.

But if a man or woman
is a believer in Jesus Christ
by his own confession,
I must,
I truly must
accept him as Christ has accepted me . . .
not because of
but in spite of my behavior.

Yes
behavior is a concern too.
I will be concerned about my own.

53

APR.
4

"... to serve God in a new way, the way of the spirit, in contrast to the old way, the way of a written code." Romans 7:6 (NEB)

For all its freedom,
the "way of the spirit"
is much more restricting than the law of
the written code.
A spiritual tie to God
makes our spirit answer to God's;
a foolproof relationship,
when honestly done.
Matching rules with "Kept obedience"
still leaves room for much inner conniving
and even stupidity about the true meaning
of our faith.
The way of the spirit not only obeys;
it knows why.

APR.
5

"You must face the fact: the final age of this world is to be a time of troubles."
2 Timothy 3:1 (NEB)

You must face the fact of life as it is.
For a Christian
to float along in an unrealistic bubble,
with a glib answer
pre-fabricated for every situation
is not to really live
or be aware of life at all.

If God has raised you
above the troubles of the soul
which affect those around you,
Praise Him . . .
but do not let your praises
drown out the cries of those who are in
trouble.
To be fully alive,
we must face the world as it is,
whether we approve of it or not.
Today,
may my faith make me not deaf,
but sensitive.

APR.
6

"Satan, the deceiver of the whole world . . ."
Revelation 12:9 (RSV)
"By the sacrifice of the Lamb they have conquered him, and by the testimony which they uttered." Revelation 12:11 (NEB)

Wrong is so deceitful.
It never appears as pure evil,
ugly, distasteful, full of hurt . . .
but it appears as intrigue
highly spiced with interest,
and just a pinch of guilt.

But when wrong is indulged in,
the other aspects seem to disappear
and that faint flavor of guilt takes over,
sickening the whole conscience.

How can wrong be so strong?
Because it can seem so right!

O God,
by the sacrifice of Jesus Christ,
and by words of witness which demand consistent
Christian living,
may we conquer the deceit of our own hearts.

APR.
7

"He will speak peace to his people . . . to those who turn to him in their hearts."
Psalm 85:8 (RSV)

The activity of a day,
the restlessness of a mind,
the crush of circumstances,
hurrying from necessity to necessity . . .
Do I have time for God?

Do I have time for peace of mind?
Time
is longer and smoother and stronger
when its fragments
are cemented with peace.
I must turn to God in my heart
not when I have time,
but while my hands are busiest.

55

"'Peace be with you!'" John 20:20 (NEB)

If only —
If only
says the restless heart of man . . .
If only I were here or there
or this or that,
or if only this could be
then
I would have peace.
. . . and so we wander from one dark night
of discontent into the next,
carrying our own desolation
like a plague
with us.

It was a time of locked doors,
of secret, furtive meetings,
of fear of the authorities.
It was not a time of outward peace.
Yet Christ said "Peace be with you!"

And if peace be with me, the adverse circumstances
will make little change.
Peace is
with me.

APR.
9

"What is sown in the earth as a perishable
thing is raised imperishable."
1 Corinthians 15:42 (NEB)

This is written of the Resurrection.
What can it mean to us now?

We are not given bits
of heavenly brick
with which to build our eternal selves;
it is the plodding daily task,
the irksome self-discipline,
the love of the unlovely,
the attention to plain duty . . .
these build our heavenly souls
out of mortal clay.

"Let all you do be done in love."
1 Corinthians 16:14 (NEB)

No,
it is not trite.
If it were familiar enough to be trite,
the world should be a far different place,
and I should be a far different person.

Why should I do my work?
Because I am a part of the setting around me,
and out of love for those whom my life touches
I must work;
and even for the stranger
who may never know more than a nod and a
smile at my hand,
his life will be the richer for it;
and for those vast undefined areas
which seem to be connected with nothing
but impersonal grind and toil,
can they not be attended to out of a love
for God, as in His service?

*"You have received the grace of God; do not
let it go for nothing."*
2 Corinthians 6:1 (NEB)

When there is in my possession some very
treasured tool,
a brush,
an instrument,
a machine,
an appliance, a car or clothing,
I understand that this thing is valuable
to me,
only as I use it.
I would be most foolish to put these
things in a storage place to keep them safe.

So with God's gift of grace.
It is not a storage item,
but a tool.

APR.
12

" 'We have a law; and by that law he ought to die.' "
John 19:7 (NEB)

Sometimes
the world is divided into two camps . . .
not the right and the wrong,
but those who are dead right
and those who live by the law of love.

A person can take a perfectly good rule
or law, and, holding it in front of him,
mercilessly,
ruthlessly destroy the spontaneous good
of another's spirit.

"We have a law; therefore we are right"
is a dangerous and thoughtless equation.
Could it have been said of Christ,
"We have love, and by that love this man
ought to die"?

APR.
13

"Do not presume to say to yourselves, 'We have Abraham for our father.' "
Matthew 3:9 (NEB)

How much we have to be thankful for in having
a Christian home background,
and Christian training!
Yet sometimes we can rely so heavily
on this spiritual backlog
to keep our Christian fire glowing,
that we neglect our own part
of the responsibility . . .
keeping
our spiritual fire alive,
kindling new enthusiasm,
lighting a flame in the hearts of others,
and giving the light and warmth of Christ
to those for whom He came.

A backlog is fine,
but it is no substitute for a blazing fire!

58

*"There, because the tomb was near at hand
and it was the eve of the Jewish Sabbath,
they laid Jesus."*　　　John 19:42 (NEB)

The setting for the most dramatic event
in Jesus' life,
His Resurrection,
was chosen just this casually.
There was no meeting of the council,
no poll taken among His followers,
no possible "will of God" sought.
People did what was to be done,
with what was available,
and for sensible reasons
. . . and found themselves making the history
of the Christian Church!

If I am making anything lasting
out of the ordinary round of life,
sometimes I cannot tell it.

But — did they know what God was doing
through them?

"You think as men think, not as God thinks."
　　　　　　　　　Mark 8:33 (NEB)

And how does God think?

Do I superimpose my set of values on Him,
and pray for Him to answer my prayers
according to
that
conception of good and evil?

God thinks as the universe goes;
great connected thoughts,
that may not seem to fit into the small
space of my today.
My focus is too near,
my needs too immediate.
God's thoughts
are the long, long thoughts of eternity.

"Never satisfied are the eyes of man."
Proverbs 27:20 (RSV)

Within man
there is a curious combination of forces.
Particularly as Christians
we feel this battle of opposing elements.
We like to think of ourselves as
humble,
simple,
down-to-earth people with a good store
of common sense,
and at the same time we secretly want
others to have a very high opinion of us . . .
above average,
intelligent,
up-and-coming people with a great store
of uncommon wisdom.

. . . And while the latter requires
that we have a great deal of things
to put up this beautiful front,
the former causes our hearts to condemn us
for having more on the outside
than we have on the inside.

Regardless of this struggle,
never satisfied are the eyes of man . . .
We always need just one more thing!

*". . . do not walk in the way with them, hold
back your foot from their paths."*
Proverbs 1:15 (RSV)

That moment of hesitation . . .
of better judgment,
when God's Spirit within us says
hold back,
is to be heeded.

Wrong
usually appears as the easiest,
most reasonable thing.
Everybody is doing it,
and anyhow,
somebody does it worse.

Everybody?
". . . hold back your foot!"

APR.
18

"I tell you this; they have their reward already."   Matthew 6:16 (NEB)

How easy it is to look for
a rewarding experience,
rewarding work,
rewarding friendships . . .
Yet,
when Jesus speaks of those who find
immediate reward,
He is not speaking of His faithful followers.
He is speaking
of those who dig shallowly in life
and come up with the little treasures
of self-conceit,
renown,
piety in the eyes of men.

The real rewards?
They come later,
in the presence of God!

APR.
19

"Let us continually offer up to God the sacrifice of praise . . . the tribute of lips which acknowledge his name, and never forget to show kindness and to share what you have with others; for such are the sacrifices which God approves."   Hebrews 13:15, 16 (NEB)

To take something
which is not a part of me
and put it in an offering plate
is relatively painless.

To remember to praise
when I feel downhearted,
to be kind
when I feel people do not deserve it,
and to share
that which I would like to keep . . .
these demand a part of my heart,
which is really what God wants
in the first place.

APR. 20

"Because he cleaves to me in love I will deliver him."   Psalm 91:14 (RSV)

Why
do we cleave to God?
Is it out of fear
of what would happen to us
if we dared disbelieve in Him?
Is it because we want the provisions
of God?
Is it because we crave security
in some form?
Is it because we fear the future?

True cleaving to God in love
delivers us from all these fears . . .
but cleaving to God because we love Him
and want nothing,
is deliverance in its purest form.

APR. 21

"But he who looks into the perfect law, the law of liberty, and perseveres, being no hearer that forgets but a doer that acts, he shall be blessed in his doing."   James 1:25 (RSV)

Daily Bible reading
and prayer;
do these guarantee a changed life?
Never!
We may routinely read and pray
every morning or night
and never be changed one whit!

But
he who looks,
he who perseveres,   *persists in something*
he who acts
shall be blessed in his doing.
God's Word is not a charm to wear,
but a tonic to take.

imparts strength

APR.
22

"All things are possible to thee; take this cup away from me. Yet not what I will, but what thou wilt." Mark 14:36 (NEB)

In our prayers
the question should never be
what God *can* do for us,
but what He *will* do for us.

We are children,
knowing little,
seeing little,
dying before we are wise,
born and gone before God has blinked.
Our prayers
should not presume to test God's ability
to answer them,
but trust His wisdom to do so,
or not.

APR.
23

"Dwell in my love . . . If you heed my commands, you will dwell in my love." John 15:9, 10 (NEB)

Love
has many definitions,
and yet is difficult to define at all.
On first thought
it would seem easy to lose an essence
such as love
because of its very elusive nature.

But Christ has given us a concept
which operates in the area of the physical
as well as in the spiritual . . .
"If you heed my commandments,
you will dwell in love."

Commandments?
Can love be commanded?
No, but the observance of a few
of love's basic laws
such as thoughtfulness,
unselfishness,
kindness . . .
will build an atmosphere
in which love will be safe.

Heed . . . and you will dwell!

"And while they were on their way, they were made clean."   Luke 17:14 (NEB)

The lepers
who appealed to Jesus
had a going faith.
They did not sit by the roadside and wait
until they knew themselves changed —
until they felt themselves to be whole.
Jesus
had promised them soundness of body,
and in faith they believed
that they were cured.

We
may not feel like sons of God.
But we have been transformed by faith.
Only as we
go
toward God's purposes for us,
as we show ourselves to be God's sons,
will we realize what God has done for us.

Go ahead in faith & try.

"Those who trust in the Lord . . . cannot be moved."   Psalm 125:1 (RSV)

Pressure without,
a vacuum within,
torn by foolish desires,
driven this way and that by winds of
restlessness,
swayed by the opinions of others,
upset by adverse circumstances,
burned by pride
and shamed by a sense of failure . . .

What place have these
in the life of one who trusts in God,
the great sure God?
Perhaps I have trusted
in some some lesser being.

APR. 26   *"This will be your opportunity to testify."*
                                        Luke 21:13 (NEB)

Were these words spoken of a time of ease?
Were they spoken of a time of great strength
and rejoicing among Christ's followers?
No.
They were for the most
difficult and bitter days,
for the most trying circumstances
ever predicted for the Christians.
Yet
Christ said,
This will be your opportunity to testify!

When we are asked
to face a crisis
(and what day is not filled with them!)
may our first thought be,
"This will be my opportunity to testify"
as a Christian.

APR. 27   *"'If I do not wash you . . . you are not in
               fellowship with me.'"*   John 13:8 (NEB)

Like a brass ornament
easily   dulled,
green from contact with the elements which
surround it,
discolored by its own chemical processes,
so we
are prone to gather a coat of dulling grime
from simply existing in our environment.

Yet who will know
there is a hidden shine
unless there is a cleansing,
a scouring to remove the accumulated bits,
clearing the surface
so that it may reflect the hand
which polishes it.

To paraphrase;
"If I do not polish you,
you cannot reflect My likeness."

APR. 28

"Then Jesus said to him, 'Be sure you tell nobody; but go and show yourself to the priest, . . . that will certify the cure.'"

Matthew 8:4 (NEB)

The man was cleansed.
Jesus had healed him of his disease.
And yet Jesus commanded him
to say nothing,
but to show
that he had been cleansed.

We have been cleansed.
Christ has healed us of the disease
of sin.
If He would command us
not to say so,
but to show
that He had made a difference in our lives,
How many people would know?

APR. 29

" 'You have been visiting with men who are uncircumcised,' they said, 'and sitting at table with them!'
Peter said, 'How could I possibly stand in God's way?' "

Acts 11:2, 17 (NEB)

Sometimes
the voice of God
is very clear,
But it is only a whisper in our own ear.
Others
have not heard the orders,
and they will not understand.

Yet which is most important;
to be understood
and approved
by the accepted pattern of thought which
is current now,
or to know that one is obeying God's voice?

If the voice is surely of God,
others will understand
later.

"Happy the man who remains steadfast under trial, for having passed that test, he will receive for his prize the gift of life."
James 1:12 (NEB)

There is a secret satisfaction
derived from passing any sort of test,
no matter how simple it may be.

Most of our tests
are not written,
but lived.
In a sense, we shrink from them
for we fear failure.
Yet in another sense,
we desire them,
both that we may know where we stand
with men,
and where our spirits need strengthening
before God.

The man who has never known testing
may be ignorantly blissful,
but only the man
who has remained steadfast under testing
can know the deeper happiness of life.

" 'Master . . . we saw a man casting out devils in your name, but as he is not one of us, we tried to stop him.' Jesus said to him, 'Do not stop him, for he who is not against you is on your side.' "   Luke 9:49, 50 (NEB)

What a rebuke
for the many divisions
among Christ's followers.
If we could ever realize
that the Christian warfare
is to be a conquering war,
and not a civil war,
how much stronger we would be!

Why do we dissipate so much of our energy
in criticizing other Christians?
Only when we learn to turn our sword
away from our brothers,
and toward evil,
will we have cause to rejoice
in our victories.

MAY 2

"No one can break into a strong man's house and make off with his goods unless he has first tied the strong man up."

Mark 3:27 (NEB)

What is my house?
And where is my strength?
What must be broken if anything of real value
can be taken from me?

The inner quiet of my heart,
trusting in God.
This is the house where I live.
And as long as it is not broken down
I cannot be touched . . .
I cannot be conquered,
for it is a safe place.
Here I can sit in quietness
in the midst of the wildest storm.

not materialistic

Nothing of value can be damaged
as long as the house of my
trust in God
is strong.

MAY 3

" 'I have come that men may have life, and may have it in all its fullness.' "

John 10:10 (NEB)

Living the Christian way
a life can be full,
filled out,
complete,
and to spare.

Not torn by conflicting purposes
or cut off from others by selfishness,
not drained by purposeless activity
or emptied for worthless causes,
not bled by the slow drip of worry
or upset by gusts of trouble . . .

Instead,
the Christian's life
can be slowly and steadily filled
with the love of God
until it is full to running over!

"I will sing praise to thy name, O Most High."
Psalm 9:2 (RSV)

God
Most High.

When God is most high
all other aspects of our life
fall into their proper perspective.
They are high
or low
as they rank in their relevance
to His glory.

A life
must be full.
We cannot dispose of all things,
and sit in a pious vacuum.
But of all there is
God must be Most High.

"Faith active in love." Galatians 5:6 (NEB)

How does faith work?
Is it only a theological term
totally disassociated
with the everyday events of a man's life?
Is it
a thing apart,
an addition,
a luxury,
a thing to be attended to when all other
basic needs have been met?

True faith . . .
How can it be felt,
heard,
known,
sensed in a person's life?
What does it look like?

Faith looks like love.
And when I do not see it in you,
or have it in me,
I doubt that that faith
is in working order.

MAY
6

"Peter followed him at a distance. . . . and Peter remembered how Jesus had said to him, 'Before the cock crows twice you will deny me three times . . .'"

Mark 14:54, 72 (RSV)

How could Peter,
who had walked with Jesus for three years,
declared Him to be the Son of the living God,
been so bold in his declaration that very night —
how could
he
deny his Lord?

In the hour of crisis,
of personal danger,
Peter followed Jesus
at a safe distance;
    close enough to save his conscience
    and far enough to save his skin.

Do I ever find myself in this position?
It is the place which tempts denial.

MAY
7

"And all were judged by what they had done."
Revelation 20:13 (RSV)

It is comfortable
to become involved to a great extent
in pride and self-contentment
over the list of things we abstain from.
We don't . . .
We don't . . .
We don't . . .

Why do we interpret our faith
to mean
"And all were judged
by what they had not done"?
God will also judge us for what
we have done,
what we do . . .
    for him,
    for our fellow believers,
    for a world in need of Jesus Christ.

Perhaps my list of don'ts is kept perfectly.
I can do this in my sleep.
What about the things I should do?

MAY 8

"The very memory of them has perished. But the Lord sits enthroned for ever."

Psalm 9:6, 7 (RSV)

Is there any secure thing
in this world?
Even man's thoughts,
great as they are,
are they lasting?
A theory, popular for a few years,
can be disproved,
leaving its followers ashamed.
A political system can seem infallible,
and suddenly its great men are forgotten
or destroyed.
Ideas,
designs,
trends of thought,
popular opinion,
all pass and leave the world searching for
some new thing; and as being in the world,
we too must search, but as being not of this
world,
we have the underlying security of those who
trust in the Eternal God.

MAY 9

"Pay Caesar what is due to Caesar, and pay God what is due to God."

Matthew 22:21 (NEB)

Usually there is not much question
as to which things
are "Caesar's."
We must
give to our government
our taxes,
our loyalty,
our support.

But many times we feel
that God is not around
to collect His dues,
and so we pass lightly over our obligation
to give Him
that which belongs to Him.
As citizens of the kingdom of God,
our tithes,
our loyalty,
our concern and support are a must.

We have a dual citizenship!

71

MAY 10

"Let not loyalty and faithfulness forsake you. . . . So you will find favor and good repute in the sight of God and man."

Proverbs 3:3, 4 (RSV)

As Christians,
we can easily take on the airs
of a martyr.
    If I please God,
        I can expect to be disliked by people,
        can't I?
This may be true
and must be true
sometimes,
in some cases,
and in some experiences.
But God stands for truth,
for goodness and mercy,
and although these may be divine attributes,
they do not make mean human virtues either.
In the end I may have to face the fact
that what people do not like about me
is due to my lack
of godliness.

MAY 11

". . . and they held golden bowls full of incense, the prayers of God's people . . ."

Revelation 5:8 (NEB)

Our prayers
are only words.
They are often ill-constructed,
sometimes thoughtless,
even asking amiss . . .

But to God,
they are like bowls of golden incense
offered before His throne.
Never let them be half-hearted
or false
or insincere.
I doubt whether these attitudes
rise up
under the guise of a fragrance.

prayers

72

MAY 12 *". . . (He) will guide them to the springs of the water of life."* Revelation 7:17 (NEB)

Service
given to God,
whatever it may be,
has a special self-renewing quality.
We have worked.
We are tired,
but a moment of quiet communion with God
lightens the mind,
strengthens the heart,
and the body is only a container!

The joy of the Lord,
a spring of living water
bubbling up constantly
from within.
Do I have this today?
. . . for whom has my work been done?

MAY 13 *"The Lord takes pleasure in those who fear him, in those who hope in his steadfast love."* Psalm 147:11 (RSV)

Fear . . .
Hope . . .
These two words depict the whole
human predicament.
They are the uncertainty of a child's first step,
the longing of the child to be grown,
the fear and hope entangled in the adolescent,
the vibrant hope of the young and strong,
the fear of growing old and accomplishing nothing,
and dying . . . .
The fear,
the hope,
they are uncertain words,
never quite enough in themselves;
But
Fear God,
Hope in God,
these are words of a different tone,
and somehow
impart a quiet confidence to life.

MAY 14

"Let my prayer be counted as incense before thee, and the lifting up of my hands as an evening sacrifice!" Psalm 141:2 (RSV)

The lamb
that the Hebrews sacrificed
was to be without blemish.
The oil was to be of the finest,
the grain of the highest quality,
the produce of the first fruits.
No tainted
or second-rate thing
was to be used in the sacrifices.

This evening
will my hands qualify
for an "offering" to God?
Will He be pleased
if I hold them before Him
with today's living upon them?

Sin of
the day

MAY 15

"Guided by the Spirit he (Simeon) came into the temple, and when the parents brought in the child Jesus to do for him what was customary under the Law . . ." Luke 2:27 (NEB)

Those who would follow God's Law
and those who would follow God's Spirit
usually feel that they must go two ways,
be of two camps.
In the instance of Simeon
meeting Jesus' parents,
we see how a sincere heeding of the Law
and a sincere following of the Spirit
can merge
and be the harkening to one voice . . .
The voice of God!

We need God's Law for firmness,
God's Spirit for enthusiasm.

74

"A righteous man knows the rights of the poor; a wicked man does not understand such knowledge."   Proverbs 29:7 (RSV)

Lack of understanding
can be wickedness.

A person is lonely, withdrawn.
I think he is proud, a snob.
My misunderstanding can be wickedness.

A person is confused, lost.
To me he is a bore,
no profit to me,
and not even interesting.
My lack of understanding is wickedness

But I have done nothing!
That is precisely the trouble . . .
The wicked
does not
understand.

in a certain mood — you assume they're another certain way — kind of person

"Fret not yourself because of evildoers, . . . for the evil man has no future."
Proverbs 24:19, 20 (RSV)

Our life
as Christians,
is a long steady progression,
perhaps lowly here,
but always rising
until someday it will find its culmination
in the presence of God.

The life
of the man who has no time for God
may look
more spectacular at this stage,
but it is only because its arc is shorter.
This is his high point!
And when he wanes in his own strength
he will find that he has fallen short
of attaining God's presence.

Fret yourself?
Perhaps with sorrow for him,
but not with envy.

*". . . each of you must be quick to listen,
slow to speak."* James 1:19 (NEB)

Slow to listen
quick to speak . . .
This is a pattern which seems to come without
effort.
Quick to listen?
Who has time for the problems of another,
when he has so many of his own?

Yet he who would exert
a godly bit of restraint
will be quick to listen,
slow to speak.
And it may even be that in the experience of
honest listening, some of our own problems
will seem so small
that we will be glad we had not mentioned them
. . . for often even our confessions
are pride thinly disguised.

MAY
19

*"If you love only those who love you, what
reward can you expect?"*
Matthew 5:46 (NEB)

The Christian life
always seems to demand
that we go one step beyond the obvious.
To reciprocate love
is easy.
To love
and wait for that love to be returned,
is pleasant.
Why must I love those who do not love me?

Since the beginning of time,
God's love for the world
has been
for the most part
unreturned.
Who am I?

76

MAY 20

"Let me hear what God the Lord will speak,
for he will speak peace to his people . . . to
those who turn to him in their hearts."

Psalm 85:8 (RSV)

To those
who turn to God
with their whole heart
the words of God will bring peace,
no matter what those words say.
. . . for they have made up their minds
to hear
what God the Lord will say.

When you don't feel like reading think of this!

MAY 21

"Whatever you pray for in faith you will
receive." Matthew 21:22 (NEB)

Do you mean I'd really receive what I pray
for? I don't believe that!
Well,
If you don't believe it,
of course you won't!

Doubt is easy.
Belief,
true faith,
is an intent sort of life.
It demands concentration,
determination,
single-mindedness,
discipline of the heart and spirit.
If you can
really believe,
God can do anything for you
or through you . . .
Because you'll be that kind of person.

"The Lord is the strength of his people."
Psalm 28:8 (RSV)

Every day
upon awakening
I must think of the activities of that day.
There must
be one which is outstanding,
fresh,
creative,
something which gives the day
character and worth . . .
and that thing gives me strength and courage
for the things that are simply "to be done."

So
upon awakening,
the thought of God,
the thought of His existence
and my relationship to Him,
should make me glad,
and this gladness make me strong.

"In thee they trusted, and were not disappointed."
Psalm 22:5 (RSV)

In what do I trust?
On what do I rely most heavily?

What if it were taken away?

Do I trust in what I have,
what I am,
or in human loves and ties?

Supremely,
I cannot.
These are God's good gifts,
but from their goodness
I must raise my eyes to the giver of
all good and perfect things.
He cannot be taken away,
or die,
or fail;
and if my eyes are on Him basically,
I cannot be deeply disappointed.

MAY 24

" 'Come down now from the cross. If we see that, we shall believe.' " Mark 15:32 (NEB)

Things
are not always what they appear to be
on the surface.
Apparent success can be crumbling at the core.
Apparent failure
can be the steppingstone to a higher plane.) *Taylor Wheaton*

Christ hung on the cross while His enemies
taunted Him . . .
He was reconciling the world to God.
Judas sat with his purse of gold . . .
on his way to suicide.

There is always the insinuation
"Come down from the cross . . . prove Yourself!"

O God,
help me, as You helped Christ.
never to sacrifice my sense of purpose
for the sake of what looks good
at the moment.

MAY 25

"O God, thou art my God. I seek thee."
Psalm 63:1 (RSV)

When should I seek God?

It is like the seeking
for my best friend.
When events of great happiness come,
I want to thank Him.
When sadness comes,
I want to talk with Him.
In the events of everyday life
He gives a sense of sparkle and vitality
after a chat with Him . . .

When should I seek God?
When do I seek my best friend?

MAY 26

"May his name endure for ever, his fame continue as long as the sun."
Psalm 72:17 (RSV)

There is
within the heart of every person,
to some extent,
the desire to be immortal;
to erect some monument to his life
which death will not erase.

. . . and yet most lives are so ordinary,
and there are so many of them,
how can we all be remembered?

A life which is lived
by faith in God;
is this not the only sure way
to immortality?

MAY 27

". . . there is none among us who knows how long."
Psalm 74:9 (RSV)

Ignorance of the future
can be both
annoying
and stimulating.
Surely we do not know
"how long" we must wait
for certain developments,
or if God's all-knowing goodness
will deem them good for us at all!

We do not know . . .

But if we knew,
would we still trust?

MAY 28

*" 'For men this is impossible; but everything
is possible for God.' "*

Matthew 19:26 (NEB)

This statement
has come to be the anchor of my Christian faith.

Much of the Bible is incredible.
Salvation itself
cannot be reasoned out.
Christ's life has many parts hard to believe,
and surely untrue,
if He were merely a man.
Even the life expected of me
as a Christian . . .
All
impossible for men;
But with God, everything is possible.

MAY 29

*"When one says 'I am Paul's man,' and an-
other, 'I am for Apollos,' are you not all too
human?"*

1 Corinthians 3:4 (NEB)

The confusion of it all!
There are those
to whom denominational barriers do not matter,
and neither does their faith.
Then there are the spiritual stalwarts
who eat and drink to the glory of God
and speak the language of heaven,
who will not speak to their neighbor
because he does not believe
in some fine point of doctrine!

O God,
give to me depth of spiritual understanding,
but do not let it make of me
a righteous snob.

MAY
30
Memorial Day

"For they gave their very selves . . ."
2 Corinthians 8:5 (NEB)

If we give our possessions
bit by bit
to God,
There is always a slight sense
of personal loss when we are parted
from them.
We have rooted them from their rightful
place,
and contributed them to a good cause.
Unconsciously or consciously,
we may feel that we have done good
which will surely be rewarded . . .
And if that reward never comes,
there may be a slight feeling of disappointment,
an attitude that
doing good things doesn't pay.

But if we give ourselves to God,
what loss is it to give Him that
which is already His?
And when we give, we expect nothing in return,
for it was God's
on loan to us.

Gift from God & His always

MAY
31

*". . . for she has herself been a good friend
to many."*
Romans 16:2 (NEB)

How many people
would count me among their good friends?

During the course of a day,
how many acts of pure friendship
do I perform?
. . . not because this is a good contact,
    or because I may need this person later,
but for pure friendship, asking nothing
in return?

Home
is the best place to practice pure friendship.
Having practiced it there,
I am ready to use it on those I meet.

82

JUNE 1   *"There was a wedding . . . and Jesus and his disciples were guests also."*

John 2:1, 2 (NEB)

What kind of picture do we have of the
followers of Christ?
We want to be like our Master.
What was Jesus like?

Socially, Jesus stood for no sham,
or corruption.
He hated hypocrisy.
But He did not,
for the sake of His holiness,
stay away from common social functions.
And when a fault arose in the feast,
He did not condemn —
He corrected it!

Do we not need more up and go
as Christians,
And less withdrawing condemnation?

JUNE 2   *"In judging your fellow-man you condemn yourself, since you, the judge, are equally guilty."*   Romans 2:1 (NEB)

How easy and pleasant it is to judge . . .
I can with accuracy and speed
judge why,
and how,
and with what motives
the act was done.

And having judged, I am set apart,
the sinner from the sinless.

Or does it show
that I am so familiar with the motives
of others,
because mine are similar?

If I were absolutely guiltless,
could I ever suspect wrong so expertly?

JUNE 3

"Behold, Thou desirest truth in the inward being; therefore teach me wisdom in my secret heart." Psalm 51:6 (RSV)

How often our spoken motives
are once
or twice removed
from the reason in our inmost heart!
Do we make excuses
to justify what we want,
and cover up impulse with rationalization?

If our inmost
secret heart could be wise,
living need not be a series
of excuses for ourselves.

JUNE 4

"Moses and Aaron did as the Lord commanded . . . But the magicians of Egypt did the same by their magic arts; so Pharaoh's heart remained hardened." Exodus 7:20, 22 (RSV)

Unreasonable things
make us uncomfortable.
We want to understand
God,
we want to be able to interpret
God
in terms of our own comprehension.

As long as we can duplicate
or explain
the works of God,
we feel comfortable.
We identify with Him.
He is one of us,
and we love Him . . .
    But we do not worship Him.

God so much greater then us.

" 'Is it permitted to heal on the Sabbath?
It is therefore permitted to do good on the
Sabbath.' " Matthew 12:10, 12 (NEB)

Jesus
never promoted blind observance of the Law.
His whole approach
was practical and human.
His relationship to the Father
was not the sort
which would rather take a nap on Sunday afternoon
than risk breaking the Law
by helping someone who needed help.

Keeping God's day as a day of rest is good
if we honestly do it to please Him.
But I wonder
if God is not sometimes displeased
by the excuses I make
for my laziness on His day.

"Heaven and earth will pass away; my words
will never pass away."
Matthew 24:35 (NEB)

All
that seems to be of absorbing importance
to me today,
will be gone.
  The dates scheduled,
  the meals to be cooked,
  the deadlines to be met,
  the clothes to be bought,
  the jobs to be done . . .
They will be forgotten by tomorrow
or next year.

But the Word of God
has a timeless quality,
as fresh tomorrow as it was yesterday,
or a hundred years ago.
What a good thing
around which to center our lives!

JUNE 7 *"Is anything too hard for the Lord? At the appointed time I will return to you . . . and Sarah shall have a son."* Genesis 18:14 (RSV)

We believe
that God is able to do anything . . .
anything,
that is,
within the range of human possibility.
We count it an affront to our common sense
to pray for things which are not likely to happen,
or which in our opinion
could not happen at all

Usually,
somewhere below this high mark of the best,
but impossible,
there are two or three lesser choices
from which we let God choose for us.

Should God's power to do,
even through me,
be underestimated in my mind?

JUNE 8 *" 'Alas for you, lawyers and Pharisees, hypocrites!' "* Matthew 23:23 (NEB)

Jesus
had great understanding
of all human need.
But He had no patience with those
who were one thing outside
and another thing inside.

The Pharisees
knew God's Law and God's wishes,
and went to great length
to appear to fulfill them;
But they lacked that inner accord with God
which could label their faith
as genuine, and Jesus had no use for it.

Not knowledge,
not appearance of obedience,
but inner accord with God . . .
What would Christ say of my faith?

JUNE 9

" 'All we have here,' they said, 'is five loaves and two fishes.' 'Let me have them,' he replied.
Some five thousand men shared in this meal."
Matthew 14:16, 17, 21 (NEB)

How?
How can God do anything with me?
. . . tied to daily living,
    with no time for the esthetic,
    holding down a job,
    managing a house,
    raising a family,
    providing for the future . . .
How can I do anything about the spiritually
hungry around me?

Are these all you have?
Give them to Me,
Christ says,
and you will be surprised
by what I can accomplish with them.

JUNE 10

"Since God has shown you all this . . . you
(Joseph) shall be over my house."
Genesis 41:39, 40 (RSV)

Understanding costs.
The deeper our insight penetrates
into the world of men,
    the more we feel the disparity
    between our fellow Christians,
        the more we sense the problems involved
            in witnessing to Jesus Christ in the world,
the heavier is our responsibility
before God.

There are many things
which we do not understand.
For these we must have respect.
    But there are many things
    which we do understand.
    For these
    we are responsible.

JUNE 11   *"Surely goodness and mercy shall follow me all the days of my life."*   Psalm 23:6 (RSV)

God's
goodness and mercy follow me,
pursue me
wherever I go.

But when I go
leaving my footprints,
do I leave the ways of goodness and mercy
where I have been?
What kind of spirit
is in a room
or a gathering
or in a town
when I leave?

God's goodness and mercy follow me.
Do I leave a little of them behind me?

JUNE 12   *"Then they began to look for a way to arrest him, for they saw that the parable was aimed at them."*   Mark 12:12 (NEB)

One sure way
to arouse dangerous hatred
on the part of those who are in the wrong
is to point out their doings.

This leaves us with no sense of remorse
when they are angry.
If the shoe fits, wear it!

But when the situation is reversed,
do we not likewise prove our own guilt
when an accusation makes us angry?

A false statement lights no fire.
We can laugh it off.

JUNE 13

"One of you will betray me — one who is eating with me."   Mark 14:18 (NEB)

It is significant
that Christianity began in this way.
Christ was not betrayed by someone in the
ranks of those who openly despised Him,
but by one of His own group,
a pretender
or a weak-spirited follower
who cashed in his loyalty
for favor and money.

Today
Christians cause more ridicule to be heaped
on the name of Jesus Christ
than those who do not profess to believe.

Do I?

JUNE 14

"She looked into his face and said, 'You were there too, with this man from Nazareth, this Jesus.'"   Mark 14:67 (NEB)

When people look at our faces,
what do they see?
Good grooming?
I hope.
Health?
Fine.
Nationality?
Yes . . .
No more?
Do they see the face of one who has been with
Jesus,
a kind, understanding, concerned face,
which says,
"I am a Christian, and because God loves you,
I too love you"?

A Christian's face . . .
Not a face of pious dolefulness,
but a face which reflects inner joy.

JUNE 15 *"May he grant you your heart's desire, and fulfil all your plans!"* Psalm 20:4 (RSV)

If God
would promise to do this for us
today,
what would we have?
What do I want today?
What do I plan today?
Tonight,
how shall I gauge success?

I must confess,
often I have no all-encompassing goal for
a day,
and when night comes,
I cannot tell whether I have succeeded
or failed.
If today, in my work,
I would desire to be an honest Christian,
and plan to share my faith in a practical
way,
through showing love to my family and friends
and those with whom I come in contact,
will I succeed?
At least I will know if I have failed.

JUNE 16 *"His disciples answered him, 'How can one feed these men with bread here in the desert?' And he asked them, 'How many loaves have you?'"* Mark 8:4, 5 (RSV)

Any sincere concern over the state of our
fellow man,
any asking of God for the bettering of
that state,
will always revert to us,
and become our responsibility.
Once we see a need,
and say "O God, what can You do?"
God says, "My child, what can *you* do?"

What they could do,
the few loaves,
were not sufficient.
But with Christ's blessing, they fed the
hungry crowd.

JUNE 17 *"If Abraham was justified by anything he had done, then he has a ground for pride. But he has no such ground."* Romans 4:2 (NEB)

If I could list the deeds
totally good
and without fault,
which I could lift up before God
for His eye to approve on the basis
of righteousness,
how many would there be?

How much place would I have for pride?
How much need would I have for faith?

JUNE 18 *"Let us continue at peace with God through our Lord Jesus Christ."* Romans 5:1 (NEB)

When I am at peace with God
there is around me
a great insulation of calm.
I need not rush around feverishly for happiness;
It grows in this calm.
It is a simple sort of life,
which looks out in amazement
at the flustered bustle people enforce upon
themselves
in their hungry pursuit
caused by an inner vacuum.

But when I am not at peace with God,
I experience
the flustered bustle,
the hungry pursuit,
the inner vacuum . . .
. . . and my amazement at the foolishness
of others
becomes instead a prayer for them,
and for myself.

JUNE 19 *"You must regard yourselves as dead to sin and alive to God."* Romans 6:11 (NEB)

What
in this world
is for me, as a Christian,
and what is not for me?

Is it doubtful?
Is it harmful to my spirit as I understand
God,
and my relationship to Him?
Don't bother me with it.
I'm dead.

Is it in keeping
with what I understand God to be like?
Does it touch that spot
deep within me
which people call God-consciousness?
Does it lift, refine, invigorate?
Does it give me an opportunity to show
God's love?
What is it?
I'm alive!

JUNE 20 *" 'You think as men think, not as God thinks.' "* Matthew 16:23 (NEB)

How does God think?

He can create a universe,
yet hear one prayer.

He can see eternity,
yet each day is important to Him.

He owns everything,
yet can know our small needs.

God thinks largely,
but is not careless about details.

How do men think?
We are lost in large concepts, where the details
are left to fend for themselves,
or bound up in small details which prevent us
from ever reaching any larger concepts.

How do I think?

JUNE 21

" 'He is not God of the dead, but of the living.' "
Matthew 22:32 (NEB)

We say
"He went to be with God"
when a person dies.
This is true, and a great comfort to those of us
who have loved ones
who have gone to heaven to be with God.

But this is life,
and God is here too,
under our eyes,
in our work
and in our neighbor's troubles.
If we cannot live with God
here,
we will have missed half of the joy
of being Christians.

JUNE 22

"Let hope keep you joyful."
Romans 12:12 (NEB)

Hope . . .
that bubbling ingredient in life
which is like carbonation in a drink;
giving it zest,
keeping it in motion,
always pushing up,
even if it is with nothing but air bubbles!

As long as we can hope,
there is something to live for.
Hope in God
gives life an upward tug,
and does away with flatness of spirit.

Let hope keep you joyful!

JUNE 23

"To those who pursue glory, honour and immortality by steady persistence in well-doing, he will give eternal life."

Romans 2:7 (NEB)

Pursue,
not just sit and wait for it.

Steadily,
always working at
being a Christian.

Persist,
not letting yesterday's effort tire us
so that we let up today.

Then as a special favor
after all that effort,
God will
give
us eternal life.
We still haven't earned it, but we'll be
more fit to receive it.

JUNE 24

" 'At the time fixed I will come, and Sarah shall have a son.' " Romans 9:9 (NEB)

It is true
that God promises to undertake for us,
to make all things work together
for our good.
But
He also has His time,
His own time
in mind.

When I think God is doing nothing,
is not concerned,
or is not even aware of my problem,
the truth is
that as far as He is concerned
my watch is fast.

JUNE 25

"They shall not hurt or destroy in all my holy mountain, says the Lord."

Isaiah 65:25 (RSV)

In speaking of a time
and a state of perfection,
these words are used,
"They shall not hurt or destroy."
Without these two elements,
the world would be almost perfect.
If there were no acts of violence
on a large scale,
no hurt in human relationships,
it would in effect be the removal of sin.

O God,
may I not in subtle ways
hurt or destroy those who are around me today,
especially those who are close to me.

JUNE 26

". . . they praised God and enjoyed the favour of the whole people."

Acts 2:47 (NEB)

These two statements
sometimes clash.
We who praise God
tend to do it in a way which offends others.

We praise with a feeling of being
just a bit superior.
We praise God for things others can see we
do not have.
We praise, and our praises are somehow far
removed from the things we are really happy
about, because we figure these are not worth
God's while . . .

We do not praise God to please people,
but neither do we want to offend them
by our unreal "Praising."

**JUNE
27**

*"And Moses said, 'I will turn aside and see
this great sight, why the bush is not burnt
. . .'"*   Exodus 3:3 (RSV)

There was work
for this man to do.
There was the daily job
of being a good sheepherder.

Yet when the unusual happened,
duty did not blind his eyes
or dull his senses.
He had time to step aside
and see
and wonder.

And when God saw he turned aside to see,
God called to him and said
*"Moses,
the place on which you stand is Holy Ground!"*

What
if he had not had time
to turn aside
and see
and wonder?

**JUNE
28**

*". . . (Simon) had swept the Samaritans off
their feet . . . claiming to be someone great.
'This man,' they said, 'is that power of God
which is called "The Great Power."'"*
                    Acts 8:9 (NEB)

Claiming to be someone great . . .
This never seems to combine well
with the witness to Jesus Christ.

We can only represent one person well.
Either we exalt the greatness of
Christ
or we build up the greatness of
ourselves.
One of the surest signs of
spiritual weakness
is shown when a man wants to build up
a following for himself.

Yes, I know a fellow like that too.
Don't worry about him,
he won't last long.
But what about ourselves?
Whom do I represent?

JUNE 29 *"I will turn the darkness before them into light, and rough places into level ground."*
Isaiah 42:16 (RSV)

O God,
in the darkness before us there are obstacles.
We know they are there,
and yet their shape is so vague
and their edges so undefined . . .
we cannot possibly know what they are
or when we will collide with them.
O God,
in this darkness
be our light.
And over the rough places
where our feet would stumble and fall,
turn the roughness into level ground
with Your light.
And may we not walk with a sense of the
darkness around us,
but only see Your light.
Amen.

JUNE 30 *"Nor has his grace been given to me in vain."*
1 Corinthians 15:10 (NEB)

God's grace,
His gift . . .

God's grace —
to be able to accept responsibility
without shirking;
to take blessing without becoming conceited;
to take hardship without whining;
to take plenty without becoming careless;
to give with no idea of receiving in return;
These
are the gifts of grace
which God has given me.

Has He given them to me in vain?

JULY 1

". . . words have power to build; they stimulate and they encourage."
1 Corinthians 14:3 (NEB)

What a difference words can make!
If my words are the overflow
of a heart which loves,
they will be like a soothing oil
on minds which are roughened by life.
But if my words are the overflow
of a bitter heart,
they will burn that roughness
like an acid.

My words can heal or harm;
and often the words
I use
are only a part of the message conveyed.
Of equal importance is the spirit in which
it is said.

For instance . . .
The reproach of a friend who cares,
is better than the flattery of an enemy
who couldn't care less.

JULY 2

"God appointed each limb and organ to its own place in the body, as he chose."
1 Corinthians 12:18 (NEB)

Why am I where I am, and not in another
part of the world?
Why am I who I am, and not a person of
another race or belief?
Why am I what I am, instead of being of
another occupation or social status?

Because
God appointed me to this time,
this place,
this work,
this name.
He gave me this body and this personality,
this work to do and these things to do it with
because He chose them as best for me.

If the choosing had been mine,
I would always wonder if it had been right.
Since God chose,
all I need to do is put it to work.

JULY 3   *" 'It is not for you to call profane what God counts clean.' "*   Acts 10:15 (NEB)

We
have a set pattern
of actions and motions
which we classify as acceptable to God.
When these are violated,
we are sure that God is shocked.

When we are reading a Bible story
to a child,
we insist on reverence.
The child keeps interrupting, wanting to
give his own version, or ask some
distracting question.
To us, he may be irreverent.
To God, he may be refreshing.
To us, noise in the wrong place is profane.
It may not be the wrong place to God.

I do not know what God thinks,
but I do know that curiosity is the breath
of life.
Are the questions of another profane to me?
My lack of questions may be profane to God.

JULY 4   *"Let my people go, that they may serve me."*   Exodus 10:3 (RSV)

Independence Day

Freedom . . .
What does it mean to us?
As Christians,
as citizens of our country,
as part of a rapidly-shrinking world,
what is the purpose
and end
and heart of freedom?

We are ready to hear God say,
I will free you,
I will protect you,
I will enrich you . . .
    but content in being free,
    it is easy to forget why we have been freed.

Why?
We have been freed
that we may serve.

99

JULY 5   *". . . so that the name of God and the teaching may not be defamed."* 1 Timothy 6:1 (RSV)

I know that I am only a human being.
But when I have taken a stand as
a Christian,
I am more.
To a great extent,
I personify Christ and the Christian way
to people.

Am I outgoing?
I make God seem to be interested in people.
Am I sour and stingy?
Then this is the image I create of God.
Am I level-headed and fair,
wise and full of common sense,
plus that bit of uncommon sense?
Am I fit to be God's display window?

JULY 6   *"I should wish you to be experts in goodness but simpletons in evil."*
Romans 16:20 (NEB)

Simpletons . . .
Am I ready to be called a simpleton
about anything?
It is much more comfortable
to know a smattering of everything,
to be known as a person
who knows his way around.

But this is a day of specialization.
We can comprehend this easily in every area
except in the area
of being a Christian.
If we want to specialize
in following Jesus Christ,
we must be what we are with all we have.

Evil,
or even self,
is a way of life.
Christ's way is a different kind of life.
If we know one way well,
we will be specialists . . .
Not in knowing our way around,
but up.

100

"We seek only the favour of God, who is continually testing our hearts."

1 Thessalonians 2:4 (NEB)

Continually . . .
If we were to pick out the key ideas
in the Christian life,
Continually
would be one of them.

Continually
we pray and work toward higher goals;
Continually
we partially fail;
Yet continually we step to the little bit
of progress we have made and go on.
And all the while God is
continually testing our hearts
to see if they are sound and true . . .
Not true to what we believed to be right,
yesterday,
but true to what we understand to be God's
way today.

"But the more they were oppressed, the more they multiplied and the more they spread abroad."   Exodus 1:12 (RSV)

It is one of life's paradoxes
that hardship makes strong people.
In our hearts
we dream
of a time of ease and peace
when we will feel strong and secure . . .

But in reality
the only strength which comes to us
is the immediate strength
given in the moment of struggle.

. . . and
where there is no struggle
there is no strength.

JULY 9

"May the Lord make your love mount and overflow towards one another and towards all." 1 Thessalonians 3:12 (NEB)

When Christian love
grows up inside a heart
it is not preoccupied as to where it will
be given, and where it will be withheld.
It grows, and widens,
and overflows,
reaching out like a spring of water
to all the plants within the circle
of its flow.

In our home,
may our love overflow toward one another
as husband and wife,
as parents and children,
and then as a combined stream made stronger,
reach out toward all.

JULY 10

"For God has not destined us to the terrors of judgment, but to the full attainment of salvation through our Lord Jesus Christ." 1 Thessalonians 5:9 (NEB)

What is the full attainment of salvation?

What are we saved from?
From all which drags us downward,
which condemns us in our own hearts,
which turns us in upon ourselves,
which ties us to a worrysome greed of getting.
. . . in short,
from hell, now and later.

What are we saved to?
We are saved, or freed, to attain;
To continually work toward the full realization
of what this salvation is,
through a life of communion with God
and service for Him.

Full attainment of salvation
is so much more
than simply being saved from judgment
by the skin of my teeth.

"It is right that we should thank him, because your faith increases mightily."
2 Thessalonians 1:3 (NEB)

It is easy to thank God
when we feel that our own faith has been
increased;
and although this is a noble prayer,
it tends to contain within it the seeds
of pride in our own goodness.
But,
to thank God
for the increased faith of another person
is thanksgiving in its purest form.
It blots out my cherished prerogative
to judge and censure,
and shows the utmost in concern for another.
It even does away with the idea
that I alone am trying.

How long is it since I have thanked God
for the increased faith of someone else?

"It was for this that he called you through the gospel we brought, so that you might possess for your own the splendour of our Lord Jesus Christ."   2 Thessalonians 2:14 (NEB)

In some ways,
I hesitate to say
"Christ is mine,"
for He is not mine exclusively.
He belongs to every person who believes
in Him.
And yet,
until I can have the assurance
that Christ would have done
all that He did
if I were the only person who needed
to be redeemed,
I cannot sense that personal identification
which makes Christianity a living faith.

JULY 13

"How awesome is this place. This is none other than the house of God, and this is the gate of heaven." Genesis 28:17 (RSV)

The line between our dreams
and our accomplishments
is never so sharp as might be imagined.
To other men,
Jacob's resting place that night
was a desolate valley.
To Jacob,
it was the very gate of heaven.

Whether his dream were real or not
did not matter to Jacob.
He had seen God.
He had been given a promise of blessing
and usefulness.
　And the line between
　dream
　and reality
　was not important to him.
For in the courage received in his dreaming
he went out to accomplish the things
he had been promised . . .
until his dreams became concrete realities
which others also could see.

JULY 14

"A clean heart, a good conscience, and from faith that is genuine . . . (not) . . . a wilderness of words." 1 Timothy 1:5, 6 (NEB)

When the words are straight from a clean
heart,
they are effective.
When the conscience is clear,
there is no bitterness or sour speech.
When the faith is genuine,
there is no reason to give apology for it,
or to lose it in trying to explain it,
as Paul says,
in a wilderness of words.

A clean heart,
a good conscience,
and a faith that is genuine
go a long way with a few words.

JULY 15

"That we may lead a tranquil and quiet life in full observance of religion and high standards of morality."   1 Timothy 2:2 (NEB)

Observance of religion,
high standards of morality . . .
These two must be in accord
before our faith will be respected by those
who are not fellow believers.

If I speak of love
and am a grouch,
if I speak of God's justice
and have no sense of fair play,
if I speak of faith
and do not even keep my own word,
then,
my faith will be judged
to be as worthless as my ethics.

Does my faith elevate my practices,
or do my practices degrade my faith?

JULY 16

"For your own part, what you say must be in keeping with wholesome doctrine."
Titus 2:1 (NEB)

Within the framework of Christian belief
there is an endless variety of ways
to express ourselves.
True,
some of us tend to get lost in the expression,
and forget the meaning of the message.
Others of us,
fearing to lose our way in uncertain
expression,
stick so closely to a pattern that it becomes
rote phrases,   *mechanical*
and the excitement of our faith is gone.

Neither extreme is healthy.

O God,
show me where I stand in this matter,
and in which direction my spirit needs guidance.

JULY 17

"When God made his promise to Abraham, he swore by himself, because he had no one greater to swear by." Hebrews 6:13 (NEB)

In our world
whenever a statement is made,
our first reaction is,
"Who said so?"
or, "Can you prove that this is true?"
This is healthy in the field of men's
affairs, and saves much confusion.

But when we come to the Bible
and God,
and some would say,
How can you prove that this is true?
to say that it is true
because it says itself that it is true,
seems to be invalid proof.
How can a truth testify to its own truth?

Yet,
this is faith.
God must swear by Himself,
for what greater name is there
by which He could swear?

JULY 18

"He is able to bear patiently with the ignorant and erring, since he too is beset by weakness." Hebrews 5:2 (NEB)

This was spoken of the high priest,
the chosen servant of God.
It should be spoken of us.

I too must be patient with you
since I am not perfect.
I must make allowances for your failings,
since I expect allowance to be made for mine.

Only on the day
when I arrive at perfection
will I have reason to be impatient
with the faults of others
. . . but then I suppose that I will be
in the company of those
who have also arrived.

JULY 19

"Through you, my brother, God's people have been much refreshed."

Philemon 7 (NEB)

God's people,
Christians, to be more specific,
become weary in their routine just as
any other kind of people do.
Even their faith may become routine,
and lose its sharp edge of newness.

In friendships,
in discussions,
in letters
. . . anywhere,
may we have a word of refreshment
from the Spirit of God
which will make another Christian
feel new and vital.

Of course,
this requires a daily new and vital faith
for ourselves.

JULY 20

"For out of your own mouth you will be acquitted: out of your own mouth you will be condemned." Matthew 12:37 (NEB)

We sometimes wonder
how God can ever be wise enough
and just enough
to judge every living man.

But does God judge us,
or do we judge ourselves?

God's laws are laid down.
His requirements are plain.
By the response of our heart,
through the words of our mouth,
we will judge ourselves.
From entrance into the kingdom of God
to the intricacies of daily living,
we will state our own sentence.

Do my words justify or condemn me
in God's sight?

JULY 21

"We are that household of his, if only we are fearless and keep our hope high."

Hebrews 3:6 (NEB)

The two opposites which tug at our hearts
daily,
hope
and fear . . .
hope that we are and can and will,
fear that we are not and cannot and
will not.
God does not want us to be paralyzed
by our fears.
They are only to be used for radar.
Fear and faith are not fit partners,
and what is faith but hope in God?

JULY 22

*" 'Go and make it secure as best you can.'
So they went and made the grave secure."*

Matthew 27:65, 66 (NEB)

And,
when Christ was ready to rise,
the Governor's seal did not deter Him
for a single moment!

Can people stop the workings of God?
Can they slow up His doings,
or change His calendar?
If He is God Almighty,
they cannot.

So, if
I am impatient with events,
blaming people,
committees,
governments,
church bodies . . .
remember,
God is in charge.
Would it not be more effective
to complain to headquarters?

JULY 23

"Ananias answered, 'Lord, I have often heard about this man and all the harm he has done.' . . . But the Lord said, You must go, for this man is my chosen instrument."
Acts 9:13, 15 (NEB)

How simple it is
to judge another person
on the basis of what we have heard about him,
second or third hand, perhaps.
We form an opinion,
our minds are closed toward him,
and he does not have a chance.

. . . or perhaps it has been a
misjudgment of our own.
How would we feel toward this person
if we took the time to get to know him or her?
What if he
or she
is one of God's chosen instruments?
What if Ananias had not gone to Paul
because of
what he had heard?

JULY 24

" 'All of us possess knowledge.' 'Knowledge' puffs up, but love builds up."
1 Corinthians 8:1, 3 (RSV)

Knowledge,
the feeling that I know all about God,
and how to live a godly life,
this kind of religious knowledge
is like a puff of wind in a toy balloon.
Someday,
someone will poke it with the sharp pin
of one of my own failures,
and it will pop.

But love,
the conviction that God knows all about me,
and still loves me,
is like a house built on a strong rock.
And on the day when God fails,
it will be destroyed.

Can I know all about God?
Impossible!
But sometimes I forget . . . and think I do.

JULY 25   *"You are transported with a joy too great for words."*   1 Peter 1:8 (NEB)

Is this why we are so hesitant
to speak the name of Jesus Christ?
It would be comforting to think so.

But could I say this of myself?
True,
sometimes I cannot bear to cast my inner feelings
before one who does not know their significance,
and upon whom they will be lost.
But more often,
my lack of words
does not stem from an experience too great
and too joyous
to be shared.
Rather,
my silence reveals inner emptiness.

Today,
was I silent about my faith?
Why?

JULY 26   *"Your meetings tend to do more harm than good. . . . when you meet . . . you fall into sharply divided groups."*   1 Corinthians 11:17, 18 (NEB)

Things which are so close to the heart
as one's faith
must be taken seriously.
They must matter very much,
if they are to have any power at all.
Only a state church situation is one in which
all people agree religiously, and even within
this frame there must be either dissension
or deadness.

But,
However firm my convictions are on a given
subject,
may I refrain from measuring
or catagorizing
other people spiritually, using my understanding
of God as the criterion of perfection.
I could be honestly mistaken
on a point or two.

JULY 27   *"Your builders outstrip your destroyers, and those who laid you waste go forth from you."*
Isaiah 49:17 (RSV)

There are always two forces at work
in our lives . . .
those things which build us,
and those things which destroy us.

They are not always easily judged,
either by us, or by others.
Things which we desire may destroy us.
Things which we dread may build us.
Things which are honorable in the sight of others
may eat our souls out,
while an accomplishment which may mean little
to others, may be a great building up within
our own hearts.

Does it build?
Does it destroy?
Only I,
under God,
can be the judge.

JULY 28   *"Jesus said, 'Come and have breakfast.' None of the disciples dared to ask, 'Who are you?' They knew it was the Lord."*
John 21:12 (NEB)

How can we know the voice of God
among the many voices which demand our attention?

Sometimes we are confused,
and honestly do not know.
But more often,
under the spoken doubts,
under our stated misgivings
we know
when "It is the Lord."
. . . and we know that even to raise our voice
to God and ask
"Who are you?"
would be a mockery.

Then why hesitate?
The uncertainty more often comes
from other quarters.
But God's will is such an acceptable excuse.

111

JULY 29

" 'Woe is me! For I am lost; for I am a man of unclean lips, and I dwell in the midst of people of unclean lips.' "

Isaiah 6:5 (RSV)

Even with the most sincere motives,
(which I cannot always claim)
it is difficult to be
a person of "clean lips."

Life is such a maze of kindness
and unkindness,
tact and lack of tact,
holding to one preconceived notion or
another,
without ever giving a thought to their
honest truth . . .
How can I ever be a person of clean lips?

Within my own heart, I know this.
Yet,
when I see untruth and inconsistency in
others, it does not seem like a difficulty
to be overcome.
It seems like a fault, insincerity, lying.

Do I hear you speak an untruth?
It is an occasion for me to pray
not only for you, but for myself.

JULY 30

"Shall the ax vaunt itself over him who hews with it, or the saw magnify itself against him who wields it? As if a rod should wield him who lifts it, or as if a staff should lift him who is not wood!"

Isaiah 10:15 (RSV)

In our service for God
it is easy to become confused . . .
whether God is doing this through me,
or whether I am doing this for God.

Yet the outcome
of the first attitude
is so much easier on our spirits,
and strangely enough,
healthier.
The credit is all God's,
but so are the bills!

JULY 31

"When you walk, they will lead you; when you lie down, they will watch over you; and when you awake, they will talk with you."
Proverbs 6:22 (RSV)

The thought area . . .
What a valuable stretch of our being!

The hands and feet may be busy,
doing the thousand things
that make up the day;
but there are always thoughts,
thoughts of something.
. . . and those thoughts make us,
shape us,
control us,
form our actions and personalities..

If our thoughts are of God,
they can form us in God's likeness!

My thoughts today . . .
what are they?

AUG. 1

"The vexation of a fool is known at once, but the prudent man ignores an insult."
Proverbs 12:16 (RSV)

What makes an insult sting?

A high opinion of oneself,
deflated;
a craving for approval,
denied;
a feeling of guilt or unsureness,
deepened;
a suspicion that the accusations
made are true.

When this is understood,
should we ignore an insult?
We may ignore it as far as retaliation
is concerned,
but we might be wiser to profit by it
personally.

As long as an insult hurts,
I have room for improvement
as a Christian.

113

AUG.
2

"He who walks in integrity walks securely,
but he who perverts his ways will be found
out." Proverbs 10:9 (RSV)

Each day
is spent in building our lives.
Pieces of truth,
honesty,
the values which we believe are of God . . .
These are strong stones,
able to weather life's sudden storms;
they are laid in place in ordinary days,
for extraordinary circumstances.

But if I build with bits of untruthfulness,
self-deception,
inferior materials plastered in place
with "good enough,"
my structure will fall apart
under life's sudden stresses.

In hard times,
I will find myself out.
What will I find?

AUG.
3

"Come, . . . let us make a name for our-
selves." Genesis 11:4 (RSV)

These were the words of the men
who planned to build the tower of Babel.
There was every reason why the scheme should succeed . . .
They had the know-how.
They were all of one mind,
and their purpose was a common one . . .
to accomplish something lasting in life,
something which would outlive them.

There was a strange old man named Noah.
He built an enormous ark,
while people laughed at him for years.
But he did not care.
He was working under orders, and was not concerned
that he might have looked ridiculous.

The tower of Babel was a failure.
The ark became an instrument of success.
Perhaps the difference
in accomplishment
stemmed from the difference
in incentive.

Whose name was at stake?

AUG.
4

"All day long the wicked covets, but the
righteous gives and does not hold back."
Proverbs 21:26 (RSV)

There seem to be two basic attitudes
toward life . . .
What can I get?
and What can I give?

One seeking his own gratification
will naturally be disappointed
in events and people.
Others are not aware of his importance
or his need for special consideration.
The place of
"Me first"
is too crowded for anyone to notice him.

But there always seems to be room
for one who is asking,
"What can I give?"
For the place of
"You first"
is so unoccupied,
that he will find himself standing out,
Necessary.

AUG.
5

"If only you knew what God gives, and who
it is that is asking you for a drink . . ."
John 4:10 (NEB)

Often I am only a pipeline,
a carrier between the producer
and the consumer.
Of two things I must be conscious;
What God gives,
and the need of the recipient.

I cannot always evaluate the
worth of the person, in God's eyes,
who asks of me,
but I can be sure of the worth
of the gift I bring —
The Water of Life!

115

AUG.
6

"They will meet the end their deeds deserve."
2 Corinthians 11:15 (NEB)

Good consequences
do not come suddenly,
or to the unprepared.

Are the hours of my day
lived in the consciousness of God's presence?
My day will end with His peace.

Are the hours of my day
lived with God's pleasure in Mind?
My day will end with His gladness.

How will this day end?

AUG.
7

*" 'Be alert, be wakeful. You do not know when
the moment comes. . . .He has left his house,
and put his servants in charge. . . . Keep
awake, then, for you do not know when the
master of the house is coming.' "*
Mark 13:33-35 (NEB)

A straight highway
with no obstacles,
no signboards,
no abrupt stops,
is the ideal of most drivers.
Yet how easy it is to fall asleep
from lack of stimulation. . . .

That smooth easy path
from which I wish, and even dare to pray,
with no distractions,
no abrupt stops,
no necessity to give way to the other person . . .
only a smooth highway
on which to reach some distant destination . . .
This seems ideal.
Yet before I know what has happened,
I am asleep . . . in spirit.

AUG. 8

"And they heard the sound of the Lord God walking in the garden in the cool of the day, and (they) the man and his wife hid themselves from the presence of the Lord God."
Genesis 3:8 (RSV)

In a moment of the spirit's awareness,
a moment when we hear the Lord God walking . . .
What is our reaction?

God calls in many ways,
and His voice comes from many mouths . . .
What is our answer?

Is it
    Just a minute, God, I'm busy right now?
or
    Oh, my goodness, there's God,
    what does He want now?
or is it
a careful listening
to a welcome and familiar voice?

AUG. 9

"By faith you hold your place. Put away your pride, and be on your guard."
Romans 11:20 (NEB)

How
in this world of wide extremes
did I come to be a person
who has enough to live on,
who has the friendship of others,
who has had an opportunity to hear
of Jesus Christ,
and has been given the privilege of serving
Him as His follower?

By faith,
and by God's grace
I hold this place.
And if I should turn away from that faith,
or despise that grace,
I would lose it.

I must put away pride,
and be on guard against those
who say,
"Ah, what you could have been if you
were not a Christian!"

Yes . . . What would I have been?

117

". . . Paul resolved in the Spirit . . ."

Acts 19:21 (RSV)

How are our decisions made?
Are we quick to make them in our own
will and wisdom,
or slow to make them at all?
Can we say of our decisions,
"I resolved this in the Spirit"?

As Christians,
we cannot afford to be indecisive.
Neither can we afford to be stubborn
in our own way.
But we should be firm and definite
when we have
"Resolved in the Spirit."

*". . . things that we have heard and known,
that our fathers have told us. We will not
hide them from our children."*

Psalm 78:3, 4, (RSV)

How firmly
Christian teachings and ideals
were planted in us in our younger days!
So firmly,
that at the time
some of them seemed blind and unreasonable.
We may have said,
"I will not do this to my children . . ."

Yet,
are not these ideals and laws
the very thing which have given life
shape and meaning for us?
Can we leave our children to wander in an
uncertain world,
for the sake of respecting their ability to
understand what we ourselves still do not
understand?

I do not understand God, and I will tell
my children so,
but I must pass on to them what has been given
to me.

AUG. 12

" 'I am free to do anything' . . . but not everything is for my good . . . I for one will not let anything make free with me."

1 Corinthians 6:12 (NEB)

This Christian right,
this idea called Christian liberty,
What is it?

Is it the right
to freely indulge in those things
which will enslave me?
Make me less effective
in body and mind and spirit?

May I be free
by the grace of God
to shun anything,
be it food, drink or practice,
if it is in control of me.

God is my master . . .
I will not be enslaved by anything!
Even peanuts.

AUG. 13

"Your self-satisfaction ill becomes you."

1 Corinthians 5:6 (NEB)

Does this mean
that Christians should be dissatisfied
with life?
Is it an excuse to be displeased
with the set of circumstances in which God
has placed us?

No!
But in the midst of God's goodness
we must not sit satisfied,
feeling neither responsibility
nor gratitude.

A simple thank you to God
is a wonderful measure of things, and
a reminder from whom they have come.
Did I give life to myself?
Then I have myself to thank.

But under the circumstances,
self-satisfaction ill becomes us.

AUG.
14

Anything
which makes for dissension
between Christians,
within the family or in the church,
is not of God.
The matter in question
may in itself be good,
and even holy in the sight of God,
but when in a certain context it becomes
the source of contention,
for this circumstance it is not of God.

God's call is a call to live in peace.

AUG.
15

"Great crowds gathered to hear him and to be cured of their ailments. And from time to time he would withdraw to lonely places for prayer." Luke 5:15, 16 (NEB)

In His life,
Jesus felt the need of both
giving and receiving strength.
He was ready to teach,
to heal,
to speak. . . .

But when He came to the limit
of His human self,
He knew it.
He did not give dry stones to those
who came seeking bread
just because they came.
He retreated,
for renewal with God.

He prayed for strength. . . .
How can I do without God's refreshment?

AUG. 16

"'Now . . . tell me, please, who it is that the prophet is speaking about here. . . .' Then Philip began. Starting from this passage he told him the good news of Jesus."

Acts 8:34, 35 (NEB)

The man in the chariot
made inquiry.
And beginning from the point of his question,
Philip took him on to the story
of Jesus Christ.

I
as a Christian
in every hour and activity of the day
must have alert ears.
There is a question,
and I must be quick to take it up,
and to lead a man from his question
to Christ.

This is my reason for being,
As a Christian.

AUG. 17

"'The man must be a murderer . . . divine justice has not let him live.' . . . They changed their minds and now said, 'He is a god.'"

Acts 28:4, 6 (NEB)

Within a small space of time
two extreme statements were made
about Paul . . .
He is a murderer,
he is a god.
But Paul was not influenced
or shaken
by either, since he knew they were untrue.
He knew what he was,
A servant of Jesus Christ,
and was not looking for his identity
in the approval or disapproval of others.

Is my ear tuned to God,
or to the opinions of those
who speak,
and speak differently the next day?

AUG.
18
" 'He is one of them'; and again he (Peter)
denied it." Mark 14:70 (NEB)

How do we feel
when people rather accusingly say,
"Oh, you know — he's quite religious —
one of those come-to-Jesus people"?
Do we feel honored,
or do we want to say,
"Oh, I'm not so pious,
really,
I'm just an ordinary person"?

Let us be careful of any degree of denial,
before the cock of our own conscience crow,
and we realize
to our own sorrow
what we have done!

AUG.
19
" 'One sows, and another reaps.' I sent you
to reap a crop for which you have not toiled.
Others toiled and you have come in for the
harvest of their toil." John 4:37, 38 (NEB)

Whatever our service for God,
There cannot
and must not
be a sense of personal achievement
or failure
on the part of those who serve.

Have we worked for weeks, or years,
and seen no result?
If we have truly planted seed,
God will send another man to finish the job.
He will see to it that the work is done.
. . . the harvest is His.

Have we had swift success,
almost breathtaking,
with little effort on our part?
Someone else has plowed and planted,
and done the hard work.

Let us be careful
that the harvest is still God's.

"Jesus said to him, 'Will none of you ever believe without seeing signs and portents?' The officer pleaded with him, 'Sir, come down before my boy dies.' Then Jesus said, 'Return home. Your son will live.' "

John 4:48, 49 (NEB)

It is at the point of inquiry
that Christ may test us.

We suspect that He was weary,
and rightly so,
of the argumentative question seekers . . .
Those who loved the sound of their own questions,
and did not listen to the answers.

But here was a man with a real problem;
a man to whom the answer meant life or death.
For him
Christ had a simple answer,
not an argument.

" 'Anyone who gives heed to what I say and puts his trust in him who sent me has hold of eternal life.' "   John 5:24 (NEB)

Who is a Christian?

It is possible to sit through more
disappointing sermons on this subject,
than almost any other topic connected with
the Christian faith.
Why are we so vague,
so indefinite about the very heart of our
faith?

Can it be because we have set up false qualifications,
and have seen that they do not hold water?
Can it be that we have picked out
one of the minor points, and have found it
insufficient?

Jesus said,
"He who believes, trusts, gives heed to what
I say.
He has hold of eternal life."

All our acts and attitudes are subtitles
under the condition . . .
Believe.

AUG. 22

"A strong wind was blowing and the sea grew rough. . . . They were terrified, but he called out, 'It is I; do not be afraid.'"

John 6:19, 20 (NEB)

What difference did it make
when Jesus entered the boat?

For a few moments
at least,
the sea was not changed.
The disciples were still men;
the boat was still small . . .

But there had entered One
whose presence had spoken a word of calm;
One whose presence
so overshadowed the whole set of circumstances
that the difficulty seemed insignificant
and powerless . . .
and soon it was!

Is this not what the entrance
of Christ into our storms accomplishes?

AUG. 23

"'I am the bread which came down from heaven.' They said, 'Surely this is Jesus son of Joseph; we know his father and mother. How can he now say "I have come down from heaven"?'" John 6:42 (NEB)

The claim of the crowd was true;
but it was not the whole truth.
It was a blind half-truth.
Visibly,
Jesus was the Son of Mary and Joseph.
Invisibly,
He was the Bread which came down from heaven.

God chooses to show Himself
in visible symbols
and through everyday occurrences.
If we cannot translate these,
by God's spirit,
into higher and holier meanings,
we will never glimpse God.
We will only see His footprints.

AUG. 24

"Jesus, well aware . . . that he had come from God and was going back to God . . . poured water into a basin and began to wash his disciples' feet."

John 13:3-5 (NEB)

Jesus had a sense of purpose,
a sense of mission.
He knew where He had come from
and where He was going.
He was not upset
by having to do the trivial,
the humbling task,
because His purpose and mission
needed no proof of status.

He was sent from God,
He would go to God.
This could have been one secret
of Jesus' calm.

AUG. 25

"'Now my soul is in turmoil, and what am I to say? Father, save me from this hour. No, it was for this that I came to this hour. Father, glorify thy name.'"

John 12:27 (NEB)

This
shows to us one of the truest and deepest
purposes of prayer.

Christ did not use prayer
as a means to escape reality.
He did not use it as a channel to obtain
things which would add to His comfort.
He asked
that His life,
His work,
all His doings
might glorify God the Father . . .

And His prayer was answered!

AUG. 26

"*By wisdom a house is built, and by under-standing it is established.*"

Proverbs 24:3 (RSV)

Understanding . . .
That awareness
which stands under every situation,
from the emergency
to the constant care for little details . . .

Understanding
is the great virtue of love
which builds a family close together.
It need not be eloquent;
A flicker of the eye,
a tone of the voice,
a feeling in the air,
and there is understanding.

O God,
as a Christian family
grant us the gift of understanding.

for Kurt —in our relations

AUG. 27

"*For to love God is to keep his commands; and they are not burdensome, because every child of God is victor over the godless world.*"

1 John 5:3 (NEB)

How God's Law frees us!

Thou shalt love thy God,
not thyself,
with all thy mind and heart and soul and strength.
Thou shalt not be burdened with another man's
property,
or responsible for another man's life.
Thou shalt not be burned
with the fires of covetousness or lust.
Thou shalt rest for one day a week,
from your usual toil.
There shall be respect in your home . . .

What a beautiful life
God has outlined for us!
We can be victor
over
the godless world,
because God's ways are high ways.

*". . . I did it because I thought, There is no
fear of God at all in this place . . ."*

Genesis 20:11 (RSV)

Our evaluations
of people
places
situations,
are often distorted.
We hold ourselves to be
the natural center of what is good.
If we must adapt,
we subconsciously suppose
that in adjusting to others
we must step down.

But
it is a double and terrible shock
to find that after I
as a Christian
have made allowances for the low ethics
of non-Christians,
Their standards put me to shame.

Then what can I say?

*"He will keep you firm to the end, without
reproach on the Day of our Lord Jesus."*

1 Corinthians 1:8 (NEB)

How
can I ever be kept firm
to the end of anything,
without reproach?
Here is a new day,
a new year,
a new chance . . .
How will it look after it has passed
through my hands?

If I handle it by myself,
it will surely be smudged.
Even if I live it for God,
it will have a few spots, for I am only a
human instrument.
Then what gives me the chance to say
that any day I live can be without reproach?
The eraser of God's forgiveness . . .
This makes the difference.

"I will praise thee with my whole heart."
Psalm 138:1

Nothing worth-while is ever accomplished
with a half-hearted attitude.
Half-hearted participation in our work
is more dangerous than none.
To be half-hearted is to occupy
space,
or grace,
unprofitably.

O God,
May I be whole,
not divided,
not unprofitable to God and man!
Let me live and serve with my whole heart.

"We share together a common life."
1 John 1:7 (NEB)

What is God's
is mine.
Being perfect
He can make me perfect.
Being love
He can purify my love.
Being full of grace
He can make me gracious.

But let me not forget
the reverse is also true.

What is mine
is God's!
My ability
must be used for Him.
My possessions,
His.
My influence,
For God . . . in a practical way.

We share a common life,
God and I.
But most commonly
I am ready to take the renewal
and forget the responsibilities
of the partnership.

SEPT.
1
"If one turns away his ear from hearing the law, even his prayer is an abomination."
Proverbs 28:9 (RSV)

What's right
and what's wrong
is up to me, isn't it?
God understands my circumstances,
and He forgives when I make the wrong choice . . .

So we may be tempted to reason,
under God's grace.
None of us can keep God's Law perfectly,
to be sure.
But knowing God's way,
and hearing what He has to say,
can certainly turn our steps
in a God-ward direction.

And how about our prayers?
If we have no intention
of hearing what God has to say to us,
how can we expect Him to listen
to what we have to say to Him?

SEPT.
2
"The fear of the Lord is the beginning of knowledge." Proverbs 1:7 (RSV)
"I have not learned wisdom, nor have I knowledge of the Holy One."
Proverbs 30:3 (RSV)

This is the basic formula in the Christian life:
Wisdom = knowledge of God.

How?
Is this not an oversimplification?

The more we know about God
the more we understand people.
The more we seek after the knowledge of God
the fresher and more refined
will be every other type of knowledge we seek.
The more we can know ourselves as God knows us,
the more humble
yet more grateful
we will be,
and the more we realize that we cannot know
everything, as God does,
the more released we will feel . . .
released to be part of all that is good around us,
relying on God's wisdom to guide us
through the complicated maze of every day.

SEPT.
3

"The way of life in Christ which I follow. . . .
The kingdom of God is not a matter of talk,
but of power."

1 Corinthians 4:17, 20 (NEB)

The Lord's day
has come and gone.
We have talked of Christ,
of His help for others,
His kindness,
His gentleness,
His concern,
His power to save and keep . . .

Now we have gone about our daily ways.

Can we call them
"The ways of life in Christ which I follow?"
The kingdom of God
is not a matter of talk,
but of power.

SEPT.
4

"Do you see a man skilful in his work? he
will stand before kings."

Proverbs 22:29 (RSV)

How many things
have I done today
which have not been done well?
Not the things which I was unable to do well,
but those things which I did poorly
because I did not think them important . . .

What makes work important,
or not important?
Could it be that which we think of as having
a lasting result,
something which will not be gone by tomorrow?

Will anything
done in the spirit of service for God
be gone by tomorrow?

It will be there a long time from now . . .
And even though the diligent work of my hands
may never bring me before an earthly king,
I will one day stand before
The King of Kings . . .
Can anything I do for Him be less than
skillfully done?

SEPT.
5
" 'We have faith, and we know that you are the Holy One of God.' " John 6:69 (NEB)

Faith and knowledge . . .
What is their relationship
in the life of a Christian?

Can I know my way to belief?
Knowing
is a long street,
which never knows enough
to make it believe.
When we know for the sake of knowledge,
we can never stop at one point and say,
Now I believe.
There may be something else to know, and we
cannot afford to be frozen by belief in anything.

But when we believe,
believe not because we know, but because God's
Spirit has spoken within us,
we can know.
We can know many things which we could never have
known on the endless street of our own searching.
And all those things will seem deeper, and wiser
and more infinitely wonderful,
because we believe.

SEPT.
6
"I give you everything. Only you shall not eat flesh with its life, that is, its blood." Genesis 9:3, 4 (RSV)

Restraint
seems to be an integral part
of a godly life.
God gave man everything in the Garden of Eden
but the tree.
He gave Noah and his sons everything to eat
but they were not to eat blood.
God gives us the freedom to live by grace
but we are not to quench the voice of His Spirit
within us . . .

The obedience to that small
"but"
makes all the difference in a Christian's life.

131

SEPT.
7
"The man who knows the good he ought to do and does not do it is a sinner."
James 4:17 (NEB)

It is easy to do the wrong thing
by doing nothing.

There is someone I should visit
to encourage them, to cheer them . . .
I do not.
This is sin.

I know I should be gentle and kind to my family.
I do not control my temper.
This is sin.

I know I should have more patience with people.
I do not.
This is sin.

I know I should take care of my body as the temple
of God: and if I do not, it is a sin against Him.

And by doing nothing,
I am a sinner.

SEPT.
8
"To the charges made against him by the chief priests and elders he made no reply."
Matthew 27:12 (NEB)

Jesus
was being accused falsely
of charges
which would mean the losing of His life.
He made no response.
He knew that truth needs no defense.

What a contrast to ourselves!
When we think
that someone
has made a slight intimation
that perhaps we have done something
not quite right,
we are all defense for ourselves!

O God,
give us the spirit of Jesus Christ
Who, when He was accused falsely
made no reply . . . and teach us to see objectively
whether the accusations of others are false or
true,
that we may answer, when we must,
in love, and not in anger.

SEPT. 9

"Here are words you may trust . . . 'Christ Jesus came into the world to save sinners . . .'"
1 Timothy 1:15 (NEB)

With the straightest of faces
people can lie;
to make a sale,
to avoid embarrassment,
to get what they want . . .
So much of what we read is propaganda,
or written from a prejudiced mind,
that it is hard to know
what is to be believed.
Even among those who are Christians
we cannot always take what is said
as the positive truth.
There are times when we cannot so much
as trust our own words . . .

But these are words we may trust;
Jesus Christ came into the world
to save sinners.
And knowing one certainty,
I cannot feel
that there is no truth in this world.

SEPT. 10

"Do not put yourself forward in the king's presence or stand in the place of the great; for it is better to be told, 'Come up here,' than to be put lower in the presence of the prince."   Proverbs 25:6 (RSV)

humble yourself

The choice place,
the best portion,
the right to speak . . .
These are desired by me.
It is easy to forget
that they are also desired by every other
"me."

These choice things are good
when I take them,
but there is always a whisper of warning
within . . .
"Should these have been for someone else?"
But these choice things are perfect
when they come to me
through no selfishness of my own.

For while I have been busy serving someone else,
God has taken care of me!

133

"Where there are no oxen there is no grain."
Proverbs 14:4 (RSV)

We say,
You never get something for nothing.

This is true in Christian living
as well as in buying daily necessities.

If it is easily come by, the chances are that it
is not worth very much.

If we are not willing to spend something,
to let it cost,
to go out of our way to find the best God has in
store for us,
If we are content to buy the usual,
skimming along on
"Oh, this is good enough,"
We will find life to be of a cheap quality.

But if we are willing to search,
to be spent,
to be content with nothing but the best although
it may mean sacrifice and waiting,
our lives will be rich and lasting in the sight
of God.

*"But you will receive power when the Holy
Spirit comes upon you; and you will bear wit-
ness for me."*
Acts 1:8 (NEB)

You will receive power,
You will bear witness . . .
These two are spoken with equal promise
and authority.
How eager we are to claim the first,
the power of the Spirit, and all this force
can do for our lives as persons.
But how slow we are to take this energy
and use it for its intended purpose . . .
"You will bear witness."

Are we fair to claim the power
without putting it to proper use?

SEPT. 13   *"Love in all sincerity, loathing evil and cling-*
ing to the good."   Romans 12:9 (NEB)

If my love
for the members of my family
is sincere,
a giving love,
and not a demanding love,
it will guide me through the day's confusion
of human relationships.
There is an elusive cord of right
running through the evil maze
of every day.
Love
will keep my hand on that thin cord,
separating it from the tangled threads of evil.

But if I would keep my hand on that good
thing, I must love in sincerity,
I must love regardless,
and not love
If . . .

SEPT. 14   *"Let Christ's peace be arbiter in your hearts*
. . . and be filled with gratitude."
Colossians 3:15 (NEB)

In the midst of disturbing circumstances,
we do not have to plead for peace,
entreat God for peace,
beg for peace,
and hope it will come.
It is there
quietly waiting for us
to let it rule in our hearts.

Then what is the key
which enables us to let peace in?

Be thankful!
Thank God for His goodness at this moment!
Even in the darkness, He is there.
Thank God for what you have
and ask no more,
then peace will come.
Wishing for that which we do not have
only makes for unrest.
Nothing but thankfulness can bring contentment . . .
and contentment
brings peace.

SEPT.
15
"And the Spirit of God was moving over the face of the waters."   Genesis 1:2 (RSV)

It did not look to be the dwelling place of God.
The earth was without form,
and darkness covered the face of the deep.

But the Spirit of God
was there,
moving in the darkness,
working to prepare it for the acts of creation.

This day,
this experience,
may seem confused.
In the blankness ahead and around
we may see nothing at all
but uncertainty.
But if God's Spirit is there,
moving in the nothingness,
we can trust
that beauty and order will be created.

SEPT.
16
"It is right that we should thank him, because your faith increases mightily."
2 Thessalonians 1:3 (NEB)

In a conversation with a friend a few days ago,
she said,
"When John and I graduated from college,
we were ready to save the world.
Now we're doing well
if we keep our own Christianity alive."

We may not dare to be so honest
about our own standing before God,
but is this not true of many Christians?
If we do not
grow exceedingly,
we tend to
shrink exceedingly . . .
until we find ourselves joyless, useless
Christians.

May our faith increase mightily,
so that it will not decrease mightily!

SEPT. 17

"Keeping close watch on yourself and your teaching; by doing so you will further the salvation of yourself and your hearers."

1 Timothy 4:16 (NEB)

An energetic person
with a fresh young approach.
What a power for good!

But like every other good power,
he can also be a force for evil . . .
a critic of all who came before him,
intolerant of slow thought,
drawing followers
and attention
to his new ways,
and making wiser men wince.

That energetic spirit is good!
There is use for it.
But the place it must be used first
is in the heart of the owner . . .
clearing his motives,
moulding his will,
finding his place,
teaching him humility . . .

When energy has done its work within,
Then let it be shown without.

SEPT. 18

" 'Collect the pieces left over, so that nothing may be lost.' "

John 6:13 (NEB)

Jesus was careful
with the gifts of God the Father.
He valued even the crumbs left over.
He could have said,
Oh, there was nothing
but five loaves to begin with . . .
The increase was because of my work . . .
That which is left,
is it not mine to dispose of as I please?

No!
Even easily-come-by miracle bread
was a trust to be cared for
responsibly.

SEPT.
19
"It is not you who will be speaking; it will be the Spirit of your Father speaking in you."
Matthew 10:20 (NEB)

Many of us
feel shy about speaking of God.
He is someone we worship, we believe in,
we trust in . . .
and yet His name in the course of an ordinary
conversation is often followed by an uncomfortable
space of silence.
And before we realize it,
that silence is not only around us,
it is within us.
We do not have anything to say.

Need this be,
if the Spirit of God is within us,
ready to speak through us?

SEPT.
20
"The Lord hears when I call to him."
Psalm 4:3 (RSV)

What is a prayer?
Is it a set of words to be said
at certain times of the day
before we can get on with the real business?

Is it making sure that our sins are forgiven
before we fall asleep?
Or asking for what we want?

Prayer can be any
or none
of these things.
But to be real prayer,
it must be communication with God,
a transmitting of understanding between
the supplicant and the spirit of God.
Sometimes a distress call . . .
sometimes a breath of thanks . . .
sometimes a plea for divine intervention
in affairs beyond us . . .

But whatever the prayer,
it is to be more than words spoken,
more than a form voiced into space.
Someone is listening . . .
The Lord hears when we call!

SEPT.
21
"My heart is steadfast, O God. . . . I will sing and make melody."

Psalm 57:7 (RSV)

When I'm tempted to lose my patience,
I will sing and make melody.

When I feel like being critical,
I will sing and make melody.

When I am weary,
I will sing and make melody.

When I feel empty and purposeless in my doing,
I will sing and make melody.

When there is not enough time to sing and make melody audibly,
I will sing and make melody silently.

Then my heart will be steadfast,
Stayed, O God, on You.

SEPT.
22
"Without any weakening of faith he contemplated his body, as good as dead . . . and never doubted God's promise, but, strong in faith, gave honour to God, in the firm conviction of his power to do what he had promised." Romans 4:19, 21 (NEB)

Do you believe
that God
has lead you into your present situation,
and that the dreams and desires of
your heart
are those which the Spirit of God
has inspired in you?
Then
do not be stopped short
when you look at your own weaknesses and
must face the facts . . .
These will only discourage you.

Look on
to God's promises,
and you will find courage!

139

"Cain was very angry, and his countenance fell." Genesis 4:5 (RSV)

One cannot be angry
and radiant.

Perhaps I have cause to be angry.
Perhaps I have been honestly wronged.
Perhaps I am entirely innocent.
Perhaps . . .
Well,
but not very likely.

But even if I were entirely innocent,
would my anger be fitting?
What would it accomplish?
Would not that anger smoldering in my heart
deaden the radiance of my face?
. . . and should not the face of one
in whom God dwells have a radiance?

But I have been wronged!
Is this a cause for happiness?
Christian happiness does not need a cause.
It needs only to be freed of obstructions,
and it will shine.

"Indeed anything you ask in my name I will do, so that the Father may be glorified in the Son. If you ask anything in my name I will do it." John 14:13 (NEB)

At first glance,
this looks to be a rash promise,
and one which could have disastrous
consequences.

But the safeguard
lies in a second look
at the two qualifying factors.
". . . in my name,
. . . that the Father may be glorified
in the Son."

How much danger could come of a prayer
which met these specifications?

"Whatever gift each of you may have re-ceived, use it in service to one another, like good stewards dispensing the grace of God in its varied forms."

1 Peter 4:10, 11 (NEB)

Have I received a gift,
an ability?
That was God's grace,
not intended for my profit,
but to be dispensed freely
as the grace of God
shown in my particular way.

God's grace
is sufficiently nebulous
to be a comfortable term.
But when my abilities
become a form of God's grace
to be dispensed,
both the indefinite nature of grace
and the comfort
I feel in using my abilities as I please
Disappear.

"'I have spoken openly to all the world.'"
John 18:20 (NEB)

When the time came for the judgment of
Christ, He had no great statement to make
to the authorities.
His life had been His statement,
His witness,
and His document.
He had no need of defense.

When we stand before God,
the great and final Judge,
will we feel the need of defense,
or will our lives,
the daily consistent faith of our lives,
silently rise up before God
to be our witness?

Today will be a part of that statement!

SEPT. 27

"Your strength, I know, is small . . . He who is victorious — I will make him a pillar in the temple of my God."

Revelation 3:8, 12 (NEB)

Saints,
like heroes,
are made, not born.

We think of those who are outstanding Christians
as having been born that way.
We think of the early Christian Church
as having been made up of those
who were different from us
in their ability to live the Christian life.

But it was to those early Christians
that God said,
I know your strength is small
but I expect to make of you the strong ones.
the pillars in the temple of God.

Is our strength also small?
Perhaps we too
are material for God's pillars.

SEPT. 28

"Many are the plans in the mind of a man, but it is the purpose of the Lord that will be established."   Proverbs 19:21 (RSV)

This idea of mine . . .
Will it be successful?
Will my friends approve?
Will I be able to carry it through?
Well,
I've told everyone about it now.
If it doesn't happen,
will I be ashamed?
What if people think it's a silly idea?
Am I too confident?
Am I too afraid?

The purposes of God for my life
will be established.
If this plan in my mind is His purpose,
He will bring it about.
If it is not,
then it will fall through.

What a relief!

142

SEPT. 29 *"He who rules his spirit (is better) than he who takes a city."* Proverbs 16:32 (RSV)

What profit is it, for me
to reach out to make others strong
unless I am anchored to strength myself?

To know
in my own heart
that when I say
yes
I mean yes,
and when I say
no
I mean no,
and will stand by it
whether anyone is looking or not . . .
This is of more value to me as a Christian
than the doing of some spectacular deed.

SEPT. 30 *"A gentle tongue is a tree of life, but perverseness in it breaks the spirit."*
Proverbs 15:4 (RSV)

Well,
someone needed to tell him!
Anyhow,
I only did it for his own good!
He was entirely wrong,
and needed to be put in his place!

And is he in his place now,
or does he feel totally displaced,
upset,
by your lack of kindness in doing him good?

A gentle tongue
can get the message across.
The only thing a gentle tongue will not do
is express your anger.
But you were not trying to express anger,
were you?
Was not the comment made to help him?
A gentle tongue would do.

"The wise man's path leads upward . . ."
Proverbs 15:24 (RSV)

The path of the Christian
may be gradual;
it may contain no eye-catching events;
but it must lead upward.
No matter what the stated purpose
of my particular path today,
it must have a God-ward slant.
It must be a part of that greater span
which stretches out into eternity
where I will meet God.
My path today may be only a piece,
but that piece must climb.

Then should I complain
when I have been climbing,
and am winded at the end of the day?
No,
let me feel ill at ease
only when my unused strength
tells me that the day's walk has been level,
or downhill.

*"Lot . . . moved his tent as far as Sodom.
Now the men of Sodom were wicked, great
sinners against the Lord.
Abraham moved his tent, and came and
dwelt by the oaks of Mamre . . . and there
he built an altar to the Lord."*
Genesis 13:12, 13, 18 (RSV)

Lot
and Abraham
started their journey together,
but they had different quests.

Lot
was out to find himself.
He met himself in Sodom.

Abraham was out to find God.
He met Him
under the oaks of Mamre.

What will I find?
I will find
what I am looking for.

OCT.
3

"Love one another; as I have loved you."
John 13:34 (NEB)

Simple Christian love . . .
so complex in its actual workings
that if we are to have it at all
it must be practiced almost unconsciously,
unaware of its own complexity.

It must oppose the snobbery of class
without condescension.

It must oppose the cutting malice
of woman against woman,
the climbing ambition
of man over man . . .

Christian love
must simply be . . .
not to condemn or to set up
a snob system of its own,
but to draw others to it by
being.
Being what?
Being Christian.

OCT.
4

"Open wide your hearts to us . . ."
2 Corinthians 6:13 (NEB)

It is easiest for us
to confine our interest to a select few;
to those who think as we do,
who have similar interests,
who appreciate our way of life,
who believe as we do . . .

But, on second thought,
is this really Christian living?
When Jesus was on earth,
did He confine His contacts to the Twelve,
or did He preach from the mountainsides
to all who would hear Him?
He did not ask that they agree with Him
or appreciate what He said
before He spoke,
and in the end they killed Him . . .
But He had spoken.

Does my heart need to be widened?
God's love cannot be exclusive!

145

**OCT.
5**   *"Thus it is the men of faith who share the
blessing with faithful Abraham."*

Galatians 3:9 (NEB)

Sometimes
God does not promise to give us reasons.
He promises to bless our faith.

Would I be ashamed of my faith
because I cannot explain it to those
who do not believe in Jesus Christ?
Then my witness as a Christian is gone.

Faith cannot be understood.
It is deep,
mystical,
something which natural laws cannot explain.
But when faith has been taken apart
and put back together piece by piece
so that it sounds reasonable,
it becomes just one more idea . . .
and not a very good one
at that.

**OCT.
6**   *". . . we are prepared to punish all rebellion."*

2 Corinthians 10:6 (NEB)

These words
were spoken by Paul as many of us speak them . . .
about someone else's sins.
Other people's wrongs are so apparent.

But when we recognize wrong
in our own hearts,
how do we face it?
Do we hide it,
excuse it,
call it by a nicer name?

Or come to terms with it,
root it out,
determine to have no part of it,
and turn to God for forgiveness
and new strength?

Which seems easier?
Which is more profitable to Christian growth?

OCT. 7 *"Go on your way while you have the light,
so that darkness may not overtake you."*
John 12:35 (NEB)

Light . . .
Darkness . . .
How many subtle meanings these words convey
to our minds . . .
Light,
that sense of wonder,
that freshness which comes with a new day,
that sense of adventure,
and hours to live . . .
This is a precious thing,
and fragile,
to be utilized while it is there,
For there is darkness coming,
Darkness . . .
that heavy drag of tired mind when I am spent,
and there is no more chance today . . .

Let darkness come when all my work is done,
and may it rest,
not overtake
me.

OCT. 8 *"I am always thanking God for you."*
1 Corinthians 1:4 (NEB)

Is it possible to thank God for a person,
and at the same time criticize
that person?
Is it possible to be unkind to a person
for whom you are always thanking God?
Is it very likely that you will
take a friendship for granted,
when you are always thanking God
for that friend?

Thanking God always
for a person
makes that one valuable,
A gift of God, to be carefully cherished.

147

"All things are thy servants . . ."
Psalm 119:91 (RSV)

No part of life
or death
is out of context
to God.
His plans will be accomplished,
and all things moving together
will bring this about.

Some events
may seem to be going
in the opposite direction,
like small whirlpools in a stream.
But can a small whirlpool
stop the course of a great river?

In the same way,
all things are encompassed
in God's purposes.

Even our whirlpool days.

*"Esau said, 'I am about to die (of hunger);
of what use is a birthright to me?'"*
Genesis 25:32 (RSV)

The desires
the demands
the needs of the body
are so present.

The fruits of godliness
the returns of the spirit
the rewards of faith
are so long in coming.
It is easy to think,
What I want
I want now!
What I need
I need now!
Of what use is heaven to me?

But there came a time
when Esau wept
for the blessing he had sold so cheaply.

OCT. 11

"With God we shall do valiantly; it is he who will tread down our foes." Psalm 60:12 (RSV)

Those things within me
which I despise,
    laziness,
    greed,
    slowness of heart,
    lack of will,
    crooked perspective,
    smallness of purpose . . .
are not these the foes of my life,
more threatening than any outside force?

Small in name,
they are mighty in destruction,
often too much for me.

But with God
there is a fighting chance.

OCT. 12

" 'Today, if you hear his voice, do not grow stubborn.' " Hebrews 4:7 (NEB)

We
like to read verses
which do not apply to us.
It makes us feel smug.
We say,
Today, if you hear His voice, do not grow
stubborn, or harden your hearts . . .
and then we can relax,
and think of all those who do not believe.
Perhaps we will even close our eyes
and pray for them . . .

But open your eyes!
God was not speaking of the unbelievers!
He was speaking of His people,
those who became so accustomed to His goodness,
that they no longer looked to Him
or listened for His voice!
Today,
when you as a Christian hear a voice whisper
"Do this for Me,
refrain from doing this for me,
be diligent for Me . . ."
Do not harden your hearts
For it is the voice of God!

OCT. 13

"So far you have faced no trial beyond what man can bear. God keeps faith, and he will not allow you to be tested above your powers." 1 Corinthians 10:13 (NEB)

We like
to fancy ourselves individuals.
Love,
birth,
death . . .
When they are ours
we rejoice and suffer with newness,
as though millions had not
had the same experiences before us.
We even like
to fancy that our sins are original
and our temptations unique . . .

But in God's sight,
we are not different.
We are one more loved child
who makes the same blunders and has the
same joys as the other children.
And since we are as imperfect as the rest,
He can redeem us
too.

OCT. 14

"Judas . . . returned the thirty silver pieces to the chief priests and elders. 'I have sinned' he said. . . . But they said, "What is that to us? See to that yourself.'"
Matthew 27:3-5 (NEB)

The chief priests
were all chummy with Judas,
and no doubt made him feel important,
and one of the crowd.
He turned against Christ, and joined their
evil company.

But once they had used Him for their purposes,
they cast him aside,
sinful,
miserable,
lonely . . .

If I forsake my convictions
for the sake of what others think,
they, in the end,
will not consider me worthy of their respect.

"Like a muddied spring or a polluted fountain is a righteous man who gives way before the wicked."   Proverbs 25:26 (RSV)

Jesus said
that those who believed in His name
would have a well of water
springing up within them.
He promised
to give us the water
which would quench thirst forever.

But
if our well has a double source,
if we become contaminated
by the passing thought and philosophy around us,
if we dilute the water of faith in Jesus Christ
with other ingredients,
how can we expect that water to satisfy?

We need not be surprised
if those we serve
have an after-thirst.

"Am I in the place of God, who has withheld from you . . ."   Genesis 30:2 (RSV)

It is so natural
to blame things on others!
When we
feel empty and stupid,
blundering or frustrated,
our first impulse
is to look at another person
and find in him
the reason for our own inefficiency.

We blame others
because we do not want to blame ourselves
and we dare not blame God.

Why not?
It might be a relief.

151

"Behold, the Lord's hand is not shortened,
that it cannot save, or his ear dull that it
cannot hear. . . . But your . . ."

Isaiah 59:1 (RSV)

In all of our complexities,
we rely on the words
"But God"
to make the difference
between success and failure as a Christian.

There are times, however,
when we need to look in another direction.
God is willing . . . but you?
God is strong . . . but you?
God is able . . . but you?

But you?
Is there doubt and confusion in our minds?
Does God's power seem cut off?
He is not gone.
He is there,
with His strength and power and love.
But you,
with your blindness and dullness
are not taking on that strength!

"Let another praise you, and not your own
mouth."

Proverbs 27:2 (RSV)

People
are not blind.
And most people,
in order to be accepted themselves,
will compliment me if at all possible.
Very few
genuinely praiseworthy things
will pass uncommented upon.

But to call attention
to my own virtues,
by open means or subtle,
lessens their value in the sight
of others
and in the sight of God.

If I sing my own praises,
it has been done.
No one else will feel a need to.

OCT.
19

"I have no good apart from thee."
Psalm 16:2 (RSV)

Surely
there is some good in me
of myself
and not dependent on God
or any outside force.

And what would my life be,
apart from God?

Every good thing that I find in my hand
is like a shadow.
If I feel that I can hold out
my hand
and make it
bold and clear on the ground,
God has only to withdraw the sunshine . . .
and my hand will leave no mark.

Apart from God
I cannot even cast a shadow.

OCT.
20

"With my whole heart I seek thee . . ."
Psalm 119:10 (RSV)

With my whole heart . . .
Do I?
With all there is of me,
mind, spirit, body . . .
or are there a few areas which are safer
if I do not let God
interfere with them?

How convenient it is
to be a partial Christian!
    in the areas which happen to suit
    my particular temperament,
but to be lax and selfish
where that suits me also.

Frankly,
this is the way we are by nature.
Why bother to call it
Christian?

153

"'Do not be afraid . . . only show faith and she will be well again.'"   Luke 8:50 (NEB)

These words
were spoken to the despairing father
of a child who had died.

Nothing which we face
is as impossible
as the raising of a dead person to life again,
or is it?
Do we have a daily problem
or a hurt
which seems impossible to cure,
or impossible to live with?

Jesus did not tell the child's father,
"Plod on . . . you'll get used to it soon."
He said,
"Do not be afraid . . .
Only show faith
and it will be well again!"

This is the difference it makes
when one is a Christian.

"May he make of us what he would have us be."   Hebrews 13:21 (NEB)

There are times when I am tempted
to despise those words . . .
I am awake,
I have plans,
I have dreams and ambitions and goals.
Let God help me, surely,
but let me be what I want to be!

But there comes, inevitably, that time
when I grasp the truer meaning of those words.
The time
when confused and spent from choosing,
tired and worn from chasing the plans
and dreams of my own mind and heart,
I kneel down,
exhausted,
and say,
"O God, make of me what You want."

OCT. 23 *"Through him all things came to be; no single thing was created without him."*

John 1:3 (NEB)

This
was the way it was
when God made the world.
This is the way it can be
in every day of our lives.

Certain things will be demanded of me
today.
I will have to make decisions
or conversation
or time
or work of it
or dinner
or beds
or an agreement . . .
How can I make anything of purpose
without a consciousness of God's presence?

What a difference would be seen
if we could say of today . . .
"No single thing was made without Him."

OCT. 24 *"All things are possible to him who believes."*

Mark 9:23 (RSV)

Faith . . .
the main stimulant of action in a Christian's
life.
Life without faith
is like bread without yeast.
There is nothing to make it rise,
make it larger,
make it light and tasteful.

The mere possession of faith that God will
do a certain thing,
gives us the courage to help Him
nine-tenths of the way . . .
and yet leaves that tenth part
for praise instead of pride.

OCT. 25

"Yet the chief butler did not remember Joseph, but forgot him."

Genesis 40:23 (RSV)

When we need people,
we remember them.
We seek their company
and their help.

But once we are out of difficulty,
or no longer need them
or enjoy them,
it is easy to forget they exist . . .
to be unaware
of the fact
that they may need us too.

What is the basis
of my friendship . . .
    need?
    convenience?
    or the desire to be a friend?

OCT. 26

"Following his usual practice, Paul went to their meetings."

Acts 17:2 (NEB)

When Paul
wanted to witness to Jesus Christ,
he did not go off into a corner
and pray for someone to come to his meeting.

He went to their meetings!

He moved into a community,
joined in on what was already going on,
and there,
in the midst of vital minds
and busy people,
he made an impact for Jesus Christ
on men and women of influence.

Do we
by our unspoken attitude
make Christianity seem to be
the religion of those
who are good for nothing else?

"*God keeps faith, and he will not allow you to be tested above your powers . . .*"

1 Corinthians 10:13 (NEB)

How strong am I?
Are the trials God sends me —
the intensity and frequency of them —
any indication
of how strong He judges me to be?

And then am I relieved
when God gives me
easy
smooth
trial-free days?
And am I provoked when the going
is rough?

By this,
do I not admit my small strength
before God?
I will not be tempted above my strength.
How strong am I?

"*As the heavens are higher than the earth, so are my ways higher than your ways and my thoughts than your thoughts.*"

Isaiah 55:9 (RSV)

God's ways
are higher than my ways.
They may seem out of focus with my ways.
They may seem to conflict with my ways.
They may clash with
and crowd out what I thought to be my ways . . .

But this I know . . .
Once having determined
what is God's way,
to go on following my own way
is to take the low path . . .
to be less than the best,
and to know a sense of inner failure.

OCT. 29

"It occurred to him to look into the condition of his fellow-countrymen the Israelites . . . but they did not understand.
'After forty years had passed,' God said, 'I have indeed seen how my people are oppressed in Egypt . . . I have come down to rescue them. Up, then; let me send you to Egypt.'" Acts 7:23-34 (NEB)

God
was working in Moses' heart.
He awakened in him a concern for his brothers,
the Israelites.
But Moses
became impatient to change things,
and dealt with the situation in his own way.
He struck out at one man,
and did more harm than good.

Forty years later,
when it was God's time
for the wrong to be righted,
God worked,
the Israelites understood,
King Pharaoh let go,
and the task was accomplished . . .

All that was needed
was forty years of patience.

OCT. 30

"Who walks in darkness and has no light, yet trusts in the name of the Lord and relies upon his God?" Isaiah 50:10 (RSV)

Who walks with God
and walks in darkness?

Impossible!

Either the sense of communion
has been broken
by some other claim,
or the darkness is a passageway
to light.

There can be no endless darkness
in God's company.

158

OCT. 31

"Blessed are the men whose strength is in thee. . . . They go from strength to strength."
Psalm 84:5, 7 (RSV)

From strength to strength . . .

I am tired,
without energy.
My heart turns to God in a moment of thanks
and there is a surge of renewal!

At times,
it is not work which exhausts my strength.
It is the small pinched attitudes,
the fever of wanting,
the weariness of wondering when it is not mine
to know . . .
But when my mind is turned toward God,
the greatness of His power
lifts my heart above such destruction,
and I am freed
to go on to the next
Strength Station,
invigorated!

NOV. 1

"Keep my commandments, and live."
Proverbs 4:4 (RSV)

Live it up,
we say,
and by this we usually mean
the breaking of the commandments of God.
But what is the end of this?
How alive do we feel?
How vital?
How full of purpose?
How strong?

Are God's commandments
fetters to be broken,
or chains to anchor us firmly
to God's strength?
If I am steadied by God's commandments,
I am free to be useful,
to be creative,
to live!

159

". . . and this (our) brother is dead . . ."
Genesis 44:20 (RSV)

Everything Joseph's brothers said
was true.
They had a father,
they had another brother,
the father was old . . .
The whole story was accurate
except ·
for one detail
"and our brother is dead."
Did they not know that they had sold him?

Details!
one untrue
unconfessed
detail!
How could they know
that in that one unconfessed bit
lay the seed of their whole problem?

*"The measure you give is the measure you
will receive, with something more besides."*
Mark 4:24 (NEB)

With something more besides . . .
What is that?

It is indefinable.
It comes in direct proportion
to the extent
to which we give ourselves
to life,
to God,
to others.
It is not included
in the one-for-one rule of exchange.
It is something more besides.

Perhaps there is
a simple name for it
like satisfaction.

" 'I feel sorry for these people . . . they have nothing to eat . . .'
'How can anyone provide all these people with bread?'
'Do you still not understand? Are your minds closed?' "   Mark 8:2-5, 18 (NEB)

As soon as a situation arose
the disciples were ready
to call it an impossibility.

Jesus
was provoked with them.
They were more than ordinary men
with ordinary capabilities . . .
For there was with them
One whose presence made a difference!
How many times
would they witness God's dealings
in impossible circumstances
before they could face a situation
confidently?

How many times must we?

"Being a man of principle, and at the same time wanting to save her from exposure, Joseph desired to have the marriage contract set aside quietly."   Matthew 1:19 (NEB)

This attitude on the part of Joseph
has much to say to us as Christians.
Unfortunately,
the more "Christian" some of us are, the
more willing we are to put others to shame,
as if doing so will show up our own righteousness.

The ideal balance in a Christian's life
is personal righteousness,
with love and understanding for the short-
comings of others.
We must always remember that perhaps we do
not fully understand.
Did Joseph?

NOV. 6

"He who believes in the Son of God has this testimony in his own heart, but he who disbelieves God, makes him out to be a liar, by refusing to accept God's own witness to his Son."   1 John 5:10 (NEB)

Is it presumptuous
for me to claim
that I have eternal life?

If I am presuming upon my own goodness
and my ability to earn this great gift,
yes.
It is as brash as any other form of immodesty.
But if I am presuming upon the promise of God
to give eternal life to those who believe
in Jesus Christ,
it is, to the contrary, an insult to God
to be unsure about it.
It is as though I doubt the ability of God
to carry through on His promise!

NOV. 7

"'Do you now believe? The hour is coming . . . when you are all to be scattered, each to his home . . .'"   John 16:31 (NEB)

Jesus knew
that implicit belief was easy
within the right group,
under the right circumstances,
and when everything seemed bright and hopeful.
The disciples thought
that belief under these conditions
was the highest obtainable.

But Jesus knew
that a time would come
when they would be scattered . . .

when their leader would be believed dead,
when Christianity would be a disgrace.

Do you now believe?
Under these conditions,
the question would have an even deeper
significance!

what are you willing to stand up for?

162

**NOV.
8**

*"You are on the spiritual level, if only Christ's
Spirit dwells within you; and if a man does
not possess the Spirit of Christ, he is no
Christian."*   Romans 8:9 (NEB)

As Christians
we sometimes act as though the choice
were ours.
We choose
if we will live on the level of the Spirit,
or if we will slide along
on a lower level . . .

The writer of Romans
leaves us little choice.
If . . .
If we are a Christian
the high level of living
in the Spirit of Jesus Christ
is our natural place.

The only other choice
is rather hard to face . . .

**NOV.
9**

*"The two shall become one flesh . . . they
are no longer two individuals: they are one
flesh."*   Mark 10:8, 9 (NEB)

Do I try
to embarrass myself,
or disagree with myself openly?
Do I make disparaging remarks
about myself,
or become angry with myself?

If I do,
I certainly am a divided person,
and headed for disaster.

But do I do these things to my partner?
He is me,
and I am him,
and any violence done to him is done
to myself.
Our happiness cannot be independent
of each other,
for it is tied in one.
It is impossible to make happiness
for oneself
by hurting the other partner.

163

NOV. 10

"But when a move was made . . . to mal-
treat them and stone them, they got wind
of it and made their escape."

Acts 14:5, 6 (NEB)

There were times
when Paul and Barnabas spoke out boldly and
openly,
in complete reliance on God . . .
and God gave reward for their faith.

But they also knew
when pure reliance on God
was soft-headed.
They knew when
to use the hands and feet God had given them
as part of His provision for their protection.

Because they had this balance in mind
they were able to be effective
in spite of trouble.

NOV. 11

"You have not lied to men but to God."

Acts 5:4 (NEB)

No lie
is ever primarily to another person.
Basically,
we lie to ourselves
and to God.
The confusion arises
when we begin trying to live out
the complex motives of our lives
so that on the surface
all appears to be smooth and truthful.

We may live by a code which is accepted
as truth,
and know in our hearts that it is a lie;
We may live in a way which seems foolish
to others,
and yet for us it may be the core of truth.

In all of this complexity,
how can we know what is truth?
God,
and our innermost heart
must not be lied to.

Must
glorify
God

164

"You also are witnesses because you have been with me from the beginning."
John 15:27 (RSV)

What are the qualifications
of a witness?

To be expressive?
To be skilled?
To be adaptable,
well-adjusted and efficient . . .?

Yes,
all of these are a great help
to getting across what is being said . . .
But what is being said?

The man on the witness stand
must have something to which he bears witness.
Only the person who has seen Jesus Christ
with the eyes of his spiritual understanding,
and has known Him,
is a reliable witness.

"Unless you turn round and become like children, you will never enter the kingdom of Heaven." Matthew 18:3 (NEB)

Like children?
Why?

Children make no distinction
between the possible and the impossible.
They are not hampered by experience.
They do not know it cannot be done, therefore
for them it can.
Children have a faith in their elders
which is implicit.
It is enough for a child to know
"My father said this is true . . ."

Jesus knew our hearts.
He knew the blindness which overtakes us
when we lose the breathless wonder of childhood.
He did not say,
If you do not become as children I will not let
you enter the kingdom of Heaven.
He said,
If you do not become as children
you will not know how.

NOV.
14

"The thing comes from the Lord; we cannot speak to you bad or good."

Genesis 24:50 (RSV)

We
can make a mountain
out of choosing the right . . .
the right path
the right partner
the right vocation
the right job,
having our plans turn out the right way . . .

There is in our hearts
a desire to do the best,
and at the same time
an apprehension that we may not
recognize the best when we encounter it.

But when that best,
God's best
appears,
we seem to know.
There is no need for us to speak
or wonder.

NOV.
15

"The inheritance to which we are born is one that nothing can destroy or spoil or wither." 1 Peter 1:4 (NEB)

The invisible
has a certain advantage.
It never takes form,
so can never be ruined by ordinary methods.

An idol may fall on its nose and break,
and a man's faith may break with it.
But God,
invisible,
formless,
unchangeable because He has never been seen,
is always a challenge to man's imagination.

Let me beware
of casting Him in any form
lest that form be broken
and I disdain Him.

166

When I pray,
I try to picture some-
thing in my
mind, like
God sitting on
a throne &
me kneeling
before Him.
I'm not sure if
that's right or
not?

"This is the Lord's doing, and it is wonderful in our eyes."   Mark 12:11 (NEB)

How many
of the occurrences in our lives
we cannot understand!
There are deaths . . .
and heartbreak . . .
and troubles which seem pointless . . .

Yet
to be able to say,
This is the Lord's doing,
somehow this will work out for good,
a wise hand directs all things . . .
brings such peace of mind.

A wonder
cannot be understood.
All that we can understand is
"This is the Lord's doing."
But,
All things considered,
who could do it better?

"The man who has will be given more."
Mark 4:25 (NEB)

God
is always willing
to match any effort on our part
with a greater supply from His store.
If we exercise faith
He gives us more faith
If we show love
He increases that love.
If we show a willingness to work
He gives us more work to do,
and strength to do it,

But we must show that we are investing
what we have,
before we can expect God to give us more.

NOV. 18

"But while he was still a long way off his father saw him, and his heart went out to him." Luke 15:20 (NEB)

While he was still a long way off . . .
The father knew the son's heart!
He did not say,
"Here comes that scoundrel.
What does he expect from me? A loan?"

Perhaps
we are a long way off
from being what God expects of us.
We are so far down the road
that anyone else might suspect our motives
for calling on the Father.
. . . perhaps we are Christian for what we can
get out of it . . .

But God can see,
even though the distance be great,
the direction of our steps and the purpose of
our heart.
And if that purpose is a longing for a
renewed relationship, or a closer tie,
God's heart will go out to us . . .
Even though we are
still a long way off!

NOV. 19

"You must regard yourselves as dead to sin and alive to God." Romans 6:11 (NEB)

Too often
we find ourselves dead in the wrong area,
and alive in a useless spot.

Our God-consciousness
can be so deadened,
and our aptitude for sin so great.
We can feel alive to sin
and dead to God!

O God,
make me to be alive where life is needed
within me,
and dead
where a Christian should be dead.

NOV. 20 *"Leave no claim outstanding against you, except that of mutual love."*

Romans 13:8 (NEB)

When we are in debt
to a person,
we feel under obligation to him.
We must be polite to him.
We must pay him as soon as we can.

We have a debt of love.
This love has been loaned to us
by God.
We cannot pay it back to Him,
but we must pay it back
to our fellow men.

It is not ours to give.
It is ours to return.

NOV. 21 *"If a man does not possess the Spirit of Christ, he is no Christian."*

Romans 8:9 (NEB)

Is Christ's Spirit
really in me?

Is my first desire
to do the will of my Father?

Am I ready to make myself of no reputation
and be obedient to God?

Do I show His attitude toward others . . .
intolerance of evil,
yet love of the sinner?

By these tokens,
do I belong to Him?

"If you have a clear conviction, apply it to yourself in the sight of God."

Romans 14:22 (NEB)

Our convictions
were meant to be the voice of God's Spirit
guiding our own hearts aright.
They were not meant
to be the yardstick
by which we measure another person's
spiritual progress.

When I have become convicted of some truth
through trial
and error
and confession,
my immediate reaction
is to be more sensitive to that same fault
in another person . . .
and conviction leads to criticism,
and criticism does away with love . . .

Do I have a clear conviction on some matter?
Let me apply it to myself, in the sight of God.
Perhaps my neighbor does not need
the chiding voice which came to me!

"They feast on the abundance of thy house, and thou givest them drink from the river of thy delights." Psalm 36:8 (RSV)

God's abundance toward us
has been plentiful.
When we use the gifts,
do we pride ourselves on having them,
or do we think of the giver?
We know how to accept benefits,
but do we know how to accept them gratefully
and use them wisely?

When I give,
I am parted from the gift.
When I receive,
the gift becomes a part of me.
I may have learned how to give . . .
Have I learned how to receive?

"Blessed are they who observe justice, who do righteousness at all, times."

Psalm 106:3 (RSV)

How inconsistent we are!
At times
we bend over backward
and are superb in our expression
of the Christian life.
At other times
we do not even measure up
to the ethics of those who do not profess
to believe in Jesus Christ!

Do we intend
to witness to the power of God
in a life?
If we are inconsistent
we can count on the fact
that the very object of our witness
will be looking
at the wrong moment.

Consistency counts!

"Must I then take your son back to the land from which you came?
See to it that you do not take my son back there . . ."   Genesis 24:5, 6 (RSV)

We
have come over a long road
to the place where we are now . . .
                    in human experience,
and in our knowledge of God.
It is an impulse
stemming from good will
to say to our children
        "this is the way I have come . . .
        you must learn this way . . ."

But our children cannot go back
to the land from which we have come.
God has asked us to bring them
to this place
and from here
they must be strong to go on
into a new world
which we may never comprehend.

171

NOV.
26

Can this be said of us?

What sort of impact
do we make for the Name we represent?

Because of knowing us,
does anyone more clearly understand
the grace of God?
. . . or do they desire to know Him better?

Is there any aspect of my daily living
which would cause someone to thank
God
because of me?

It is easy to turn people against
the name of Christ by our lives.
It is an effort to hold our own
on a normal plane of Christian respectability.
But to have someone
praise God for our lives
is a high goal!

NOV.
27

"*Therefore the Lord has recompensed me . . .
according to the cleanness of my hands in
his sight.*" Psalm 18:24 (RSV)

Ours
is not a religion of works.
But even living by faith
does not do away with the law of natural
consequences.

With questions of eternity aside,
a life lived day by day
in a way honest before God
will bring its own wholesome, happy life.
A life lived on the edge of permission
will crowd one to the edge of happiness.

According to the cleanness of my hands . . .
I will be
not saved,
but recompensed.

NOV. 28

"Unless the Lord builds the house, those who build it labor in vain."

Psalm 127:1 (RSV)

Unless the Lord
establishes
and maintains
and guides a home,
those who establish it labor in vain.

Unless God
is brought into every relationship
within the family,
those relationships are built in vain.

Unless the Lord
is the center of our lives,
those lives will be
in vain.

Do I feel that my life
or my family relationships are lacking
something?
Perhaps I do not have them
properly centered.

NOV. 29

"I train myself to keep at all times a clear conscience before God and man."

Acts 24:16 (NEB)

This
Truly takes cross-examination!

We may say,
I don't care what people think . . .
My conscience is clear before God!
And we can be rude and thoughtless.

Or we may say,
I can't help what God thinks of this . . .
He knows I'm under pressure and am
a victim of circumstances . . .
And we may be stifling the voice
of God's Spirit within us.

But to have a clear conscience
before God and man
leaves no back door.

"Stay awake, and pray . . ."
Matthew 26:41 (NEB)

It is natural
to come to God with our ideas and pray for
His approval.
Yet if we really listen while we pray,
God often reveals the flatness of our own words
to us as they come from our lips.

How should we pray, if we are not to sell
our ideas to God?
The prayers of Jesus in the garden of Gethsemane
are an interesting pattern to follow
in the seeking of God's ideas.

Let this cup pass . . . but do Thy will.
If it is not possible to let this cup pass . . .
Thy will be done.
Thy will be done!

Jesus recognized the Father's will
as He prayed.

*" 'How blest you are, when you suffer insults
. . . for my sake.' "* Matthew 5:11 (NEB)

It is human nature
to worry when we are not accepted by others.
We want to be understood,
to make what we have to say sound reasonable.
We shy away from making statements which will
make us stand out as different.

But as Christians
perhaps we should be concerned when we
are
understood by everyone.
When those who are not Christian
can see eye to eye with us on every subject,
perhaps we need to check our focus.
Where are we looking?
What is our goal?
Whose approval are we seeking?
Is there anything deeper about our insight
because we are Christian?

Take care
when all men can understand.

" 'We count those happy who stood firm . . .' "
James 5:11 (NEB)

In the past
or around us,
we see certain people
who have those qualities which we envy.
They seem to personify
useful happy Christian living.

How does this come to them?
What is the source of their happiness,
and the secret of their usefulness?
Are they those who have never had
any hardships?

No,
to the contrary
they are usually those who have learned
happiness from knowing sadness,
and usefulness
from coming to a sense of their own
uselessness.
They are the men and women
who have learned to stand firm
when the wind is blowing hard,
and they have become strong trees in God's
forest.

"Therefore confess your sins to one another,
. . . and then you will be healed."
James 5:16 (NEB)

I can
confess my sins to God
and be assured that He forgives
and cleanses.
This I must do . . .

Yet
having cleared my heart before God,
is there not yet a guilt,
an obligation,
a lack of wholeness within me?
What is God's forgiveness?
Is it the Christian form of escaping
the reality
that a man must make things right
with his brother?

It was never intended to be so!

DEC. 4

"We must throw off . . . every sin to which we cling, and run with resolution the race for which we are entered."

Hebrews 12:1 (NEB)

Faith in Jesus Christ
always seems to call for double action . . .
Repent and believe . . .
lay down evil and take up good . . .

throw off every sin, and run with resolution.
The command is never one-sided,
never intended to make us empty
with no refilling.

What are the sins which weigh me down?
Are they little things,
like selfishness and ingratitude . . .
Things not big enough to totally disqualify
me for the race,
but annoying enough to slow me to a walk?
Then let me lay them aside . . .
not because the Christian life says
I must get rid of things,
but so I will be able to run!

DEC. 5

"Stand up to the devil and he will turn and run. Come close to God, and he will come close to you."   James 4:8 (NEB)

Are we entirely
at the mercy of God
or the devil,
mere pawns in the game of the universe?
Perhaps this is too large a question
for us to answer with a simple
yes or no.

But there are occasions
when we play the part
of the irresponsible fool
and blame the result on the greater powers.
What is to be will be,
we say,
and lean over backwards to fall into evil.

We know we do not have the absolute power
of our lives in our own hands.
We cannot say if we will live or die.
But if the spirit within us determines
to come close to God,
has He not promised to come close to us?

DEC.
6
". . . the liberty and splendour of the children
of God." Romans 8:21 (NEB)

What is liberty?
Is it not the freedom to do as I choose,
to be as I would like to be?

But in my natural human state
this is not possible.
I choose, and live the opposite.
I aim, and deny my own aims.
By nature,
liberty is impossible for me.
I do not have the power to be free.

This splendid picture I have
of what I would like to be
can only be mine as a child of God
living in obedience to His Spirit.

Then the splendor of freedom is mine.

DEC.
7
"Thou dost make him glad with the joy of
thy presence." Psalm 21:6 (RSV)

God is near me . . .
Am I tired?
He is strength.

Am I upset?
He is peace.

Am I weak-willed?
He is a stay.

Am I worried?
He is assurance.

Am I aimless?
He is purpose.

He is present.
He is joy.
He makes me glad
with the joy of His presence!

May these thoughts fill my mind today.

DEC. 8   *" 'It is not the healthy that need a doctor but the sick . . .' "*   Mark 2:17 (NEB)

Where do I feel most secure?

With Christians, of course.
They think and feel and react
in the same pattern as I do,
and I can be assured of acceptance by them.

But is this what Christ would have?
Would He have me
exchanging religious recipes with Christians
when some have not even tasted
the Bread of Life?

Perhaps
every conversation
does not need to be a comfortable one for me.
Perhaps it would be better
to speak more frequently with one
who does not understand me,
or Jesus Christ.
To have Him accepted
is a higher goal.

DEC. 9   *" 'The Sabbath was made for the sake of man.' "*   Mark 2:27 (NEB)

The sabbath
Sunday
The Lord's Day . . .
by whatever name we choose to call it . . .
Is it not too small a portion
of each week to give to God?
Do we not owe Him more?

It is too small a share
if we view it as a time isolated to itself . . .
the ragged end of one week,
and the breather before we plunge into the
rush of the next . . .
But if we can view this one day in seven
as a check-point,
a place in which we stop to rest
and see if we are headed in the right direction
for the week ahead . . .
it is not too small.
It makes the rest of God's week larger.

178

"For all the gods of the peoples are idols;
but the Lord made the heavens."

Psalm 96:5 (RSV)

A bent little woman,
clean,
with work-worn hands stretched out
before a carved statue . . .

What were her prayers?
I do not know, for I could not understand
her words . . .
But the earnestness,
the sincerity of her voice as she prayed
were they not wasted on its
blank bronze stare?

I wish with all my heart I could say no.
But I must believe that her prayers
are unheard,
or Jesus Christ need not have died!

And believing this,
are my prayers for that woman as earnest
as are her prayers to the idol?

"The Lord is faithful in all his words, and
gracious in all his deeds."

Psalm 145:13 (RSV)

Gracious in all His deeds . . .
Am I?

Oh, but people can be so annoying!
Why
should I break my neck
to be gracious
to them?

I wonder what would happen
if God took this attitude toward me?
Gracious
in all His deeds . . .
Not only to the deserving and grateful,
but to the unjust
and ungrateful —
me.

179

**DEC.
12**

"You have lived on earth in wanton luxury . . ."   James 5:5 (NEB)

Not me, I say
and read on to something
more appropriate.
But it may be
that I should reflect on luxury
for by the world's average,
am I not living
in it?

I don't worry
about moth
and tarnish
destroying the things I use . . .
it's the things
I lay aside
which are affected by these.

If it's possible
to take too many of God's gifts
and closet them,
perhaps
I should thank God
for moth and tarnish.

**DEC.
13**

"They will come to see for themselves that you live good lives."
1 Peter 2:12 (NEB)

Christianity
does not need to be pushed
if it is peddled properly.
If I live next to a man
and constantly hint about church attendance
and Sunday observance
and my list of don'ts,
I am more likely than not
turning him away from belief in Jesus Christ.

But if he can see for himself
that my life is good,
that I have something which he feels lacking,
he will want it . . .
He will want it as surely
as a man wants to discard an old worn coat
when he sees a newer warmer one.
. . . and this is the time
to mention the name
of Jesus Christ!

DEC. 14

"He makes a pit, digging it out, and falls into the hole which he has made. His mischief returns upon his own head."

Psalm 7:15, 16 (RSV)

Very rarely
can we do evil
without becoming evil.
We have the idea that a word spoken is gone . . .
It may wound another, but we are rid of it.
But the attitude which bore that word . . .
has it not left its mark deep within us?

If we criticize constantly,
we find ourselves growing sour
and a bit apprehensive
that others may be criticizing us.

If we are negative and demanding,
we find others responding negatively . . .
and the demanding attitude
comes falling back on our own heads!

We cannot do, and be done with it.
As we do, so we become.

DEC. 15

". . . It is God also who has set his seal upon us." 2 Corinthians 1:22 (NEB)

God's seal!
We are chosen by Him,
approved by Him,
passed,
as fit for His service.
From now on,
we represent His company.

A manufactured item
often has the seal of the company on it.
This is the assurance
that the producer
will stand behind the product.
With God's stamp on us,
we represent
the surest company in the universe!

DEC. 16   *"Though you have a name for being alive, you are dead."*   Revelation 3:1 (NEB)

We
as Christians
have a name.
People look to us as representatives of
eternal life,
of God's life.

Yet how many times are we dead inside ourselves?
Dead to the needs of those around us,
dead in our sensitivity to God and His Word,
dead in our sense of responsibility
toward God,
dead in the area of genuine inner joy?

Awake,
and stir up what is still within you
even though it is on the point of death . . .
For if we are dead,
the world is dead indeed!

DEC. 17   *"While they were . . . offering worship to the Lord, the Holy Spirit said . . ."*
Acts 13:2 (NEB)

As followers of Jesus Christ,
we want to hear the voice of God's Spirit
directing our way.

But when there is a sound within us
saying this is the way,
how can we be sure that the voice
is that of God's Spirit,
and not the whisperings of our own heart,
the affirmation of our own desires?

While the early Christians were worshiping . . .
in a submissive state of heart and mind
before God,
the Holy Spirit spoke.

This idea we are pondering . . .
In what frame of mind was it conceived?

DEC. 18   *"I will walk with integrity of heart within my house."*   Psalm 101:2 (RSV)

Many of us
can have integrity of heart before others . . .
In a group of believers,
in prayer meetings . . .
in the places which we connect with integrity,

But the kind of integrity
which is valuable in the sight of God
and needed in this world
is that which is practiced
in our own personal lives . . .
in our home
before our family members,
within our own hearts . . .
And even practiced
where integrity may seem to be out of context!

True integrity
is the sort which would be practiced
whether anyone were looking or not!

DEC. 19   *"Be content with what you have. . . .'The Lord is my helper, I will not fear; what can man do to me?'"*   Hebrews 13:5, 6 (NEB)

If I would be content,
I cannot set my heart on acquiring more
than I have . . .
more prestige
more possessions
more money or power . . .

If I would be content,
I cannot set my heart on grasping
what I have now . . .

If I would know the contentment of those
who do not fear because they trust in God,
my prayer must be,

O God,
for what you will give me, I am grateful.
For the things you take from me, I will
thank you for the time I had them.

Since God arranges my affairs,
I will be content.

DEC. 20

"The man who comes to me I will never turn away."   John 6:37 (NEB)

Initially
or daily,
we never need fear
being snubbed by God.
He is always ready to listen,
always ready to be our source of power
and inspiration.

Then why are we so slow
to come to God with our problems?
Could it be
that we doubt the worth of God's help?
Do we simply forget that He is there?

Or are
We
too busy?

DEC. 21

"But the man who looks closely into the perfect law . . . and who lives in its company, does not forget what he hears, but acts upon it . . ."   James 1:25 (NEB)

Will looking into God's Word give us happiness?
Looking
will not.
It will only embarrass us to see how much less
we are than God expects us to be.
But when we take those words of God
out of the hiding place of their pages
and carry them about in our company,
in our minds,
in our plans,
we begin unconsciously to conform our minds
to fit their pattern.
And since our minds become re-formed
our actions do likewise . . .
and to our amazement,
we find that the acting out of God's
expectations for us
brings about great human happiness . . .
no matter how impossible they sounded
in the beginning!

"He delivered us . . .
He will deliver us . . .
He will continue to deliver us . . ."
2 Corinthians 1:10, 11 (NEB)

I quit!
I've tried my best to live as God expects
me to,
as my family expects me to . . .
I want to do the best, but I always fail.
I give up!
There's no use trying!
I just fail . . .

I?

"Rely not on ourselves, but on God . . .
He delivered us,
He will deliver us,
He will continue to deliver us . . ."
Again and again and again,
like food,
like sleep,
so God will give us strength every day.

"The eyes of the Lord are toward the right-
eous, and his ears toward their cry."
Psalm 34:15 (RSV)

How
do I regard the fact
that the Lord's eye is upon me,
and that His ear is turned toward me?

Is it a promise
or a threat?
Does it make me uncomfortable
or give hope?
Does it help me justify my actions
or does it condemn me?

The fact is the same . . .
The Lord's eyes are upon me.
It is a neutral statement,
neither a promise or a threat
in itself.
The difference lies within
me.

DEC.
24

"For myself, I set no store by life; I only want to finish the race, and complete the task which the Lord Jesus assigned to me, of bearing my testimony to the gospel of God's grace."

Acts 20:24 (NEB)

"I want only to finish the race."
These words fit in well with our life.
Day after day,
we *race* from morning until night.
We can only find quiet in these circumstances
when we expect
to run
and race
until we complete the task Christ has given us.
What of those who race for nothing?

DEC.
25

Christmas Day

"For God so loved the world . . ."

John 3:16

I look across the crowded street where walks
the mob,
the poor,
the sad,
the driven hard,
the Christless mob,
and find that I must give a share . . .
and so I do, with sympathy,
and satisfied,
I turn away.

But what is this? This great high heap of cluttered things
so large it blocks my view of heaven?
Is this the store that I have left?

Then I must look
and look again across the crowd,
and never rest
until the sum of what I give
at least can balance what I keep.

And this small share now let me use with gratitude,
not as my own,
and with no smothered, martyred air.
God gave the world His only Son,
and not the one He had to spare.

DEC. 26

"If our conscience does not condemn us, then we can approach God with confidence, and obtain from him whatever we ask."

1 John 3:21 (NEB)

Does my heart condemn me
for any reason?
Then my confidence
that God will hear and answer my prayer
is undermined.
The result of this
is a disinterest in prayer.
The conversation has become a monologue.

Only the clearing up
of that condemning thing
of which I am conscious
will renew my spiritual vitality.

DEC. 27

"We who teach shall ourselves be judged with greater strictness."   James 3:1 (NEB)

If we choose
to make no claim,
no statement,
no profession of faith in Jesus Christ,
we have nothing to live up to.

If we do not speak out for Jesus Christ
we do not need to be consistent with that speech
in order to avoid being called hypocrites.
if we claim to be nothing,
we have no necessity to be anything.

But
once having spoken out
as witnesses to the saving and transforming
power of Jesus Christ,
every act of ours will be judged
in the light of our own words.

Can we live as we speak?

DEC. 28 *"Where little has been forgiven, little love is shown."* Luke 7:47 (NEB)

When we come to God
to confess our sins,
we are usually a combination
of the Pharisee and the Publican.
We know better than to declare ourselves
sinless before God,
as the Pharisee did,
yet we cannot stoop any lower than saying,
God,
be merciful to me a sinner
even though my sins are not as bad as other
men's . . .
. . . and having refused to look into the
depths of ourselves,
we also refuse to receive the joy of full
pardon!

Let us realize the extent
to which we have been forgiven,
that we may know the extent of our debt
of love!

DEC. 29 *"Fear not, for I am with you, be not dismayed, for I am your God; I will strengthen you, I will help you, I will uphold you with my victorious right hand."* Isaiah 41:10 (RSV)

If we expect God to fulfill this promise
to us as His present day servants,
we must be wary of these attitudes,
consciously or unconsciously . . .

". . . don't be afraid . . . you have chosen a job
for which you are well suited,
don't be discouraged . . . for the task is
well worth your best efforts.
In your work itself you will find strength.
You will surely be a success,
because people believe in you . . ."

All fine attitudes,
but hardly enough for a Christian's task!

DEC. 30

"I lie down and sleep; I wake again, for the Lord sustains me."   Psalm   3:5   (RSV)

Day follows day,
week follows week
and month follows month . . .
How quickly a year is past!

Today,
it is time for looking back,
a time for remembering,
a time for counting God's goodnesses;
a time for looking back over a pathway
which is still as glowing
as when we first glimpsed it.
For the Lord has sustained us!

DEC. 31

"It would have been better for us to serve the Egyptians than to die in the wilderness."
Exodus 14:12 (RSV)

Our fears
are always more terrible in prospect
than our worst experiences in retrospect.

The Israelites knew well
the awful bondage of Egypt.
They had pleaded with God for deliverance.
Yet
when that deliverance was not clear to them,
when it demanded faith
and bravery
and just plain plugging away,
they were more willing to turn back
to the terrible known
than to go on
to the fearful unknown.

They forgot that in that unknown
was God's hand.

SCRIPTURAL INDEX

Scriptural Index

LUKE

5:15, 16 .... Aug. 15
7:47 .... Dec. 28
8:50 .... Oct. 21
9:49, 50 .... May 1
15:20 .... Nov. 18
17:14 .... Apr. 24
19:17 .... Mar. 22
21:13 .... Apr. 26
23:23 .... Mar. 30

JOHN

1:3 .... Oct. 23
1:36 .... Jan. 28
2:1, 2 .... June 1
3:5, 6 .... Jan. 31
3:16 .... Dec. 25
3:27 .... Jan. 27
4:10 .... Aug. 5
4:37, 38 .... Aug. 19
4:48, 49 .... Aug. 20
5:24 .... Aug. 21
5:30 .... Feb. 22
6:13 .... Sept. 18
6:19, 20 .... Aug. 22
6:37 .... Dec. 20
6:42 .... Aug. 23
6:69 .... Sept. 5
7:23, 24 .... Feb. 12
8:51 .... Feb. 21
9:41 .... Feb. 11
10:10 .... May 3
11:15 .... Feb. 27
12:27 .... Aug. 25
12:35 .... Oct. 7
13:3-5 .... Aug. 24
13:8 .... Apr. 27
13:34 .... Oct. 3
14:13 .... Sept. 24
14:27 .... Mar. 4
15:9, 10 .... Apr. 23
15:12 .... Feb. 26
15:27 .... Nov. 12
16:31 .... Nov. 7
18:20 .... Sept. 26
19:7 .... Mar. 23
19:7 .... Apr. 12
19:42 .... Apr. 14
20:9 .... Mar. 27
20:20 .... Apr. 8
21:6 .... Feb. 25
21:12 .... July 28

ACTS

1:8 .... Sept. 12
2:47 .... June 26
5:4 .... Nov. 11
7:23-34 .... Oct. 29
8:9 .... June 28
8:34, 35 .... Aug. 16

9:13, 15 .... July 23
10:15 .... July 3
11:2, 17 .... Apr. 29
12:9-11 .... Mar. 10
13:2 .... Dec. 17
13:9, 10 .... Mar. 9
14:5, 6 .... Nov. 10
14:22 .... Mar. 8
17:2 .... Oct. 26
17:25 .... Jan. 17
18:9, 10 .... Jan. 25
19:21 .... Aug. 10
20:24 .... Dec. 24
21:5 .... Feb. 18
22:13-21 .... Jan. 14
23:1 .... Jan. 12
24:16 .... Nov. 29
26:28, 29 .... Jan. 15
28:4, 6 .... Aug. 17

ROMANS

1:5 .... Feb. 17
1:16, 17 .... Jan. 11
2:1 .... Mar. 6
2:1 .... June 2
2:7 .... June 23
4:2 .... June 17
4:19, 21 .... Sept. 22
5:1 .... June 18
6:11 .... June 19
6:11 .... Nov. 19
7:6 .... Apr. 4
8:9 .... Nov. 8
8:9 .... Nov. 21
8:21 .... Dec. 6
9:9 .... June 24
9:17 .... Jan. 10
10:2-4 .... Mar. 7
11:13 .... Jan. 1
11:20 .... Aug. 9
12:2 .... Feb. 19
12:9 .... Mar. 26
12:9 .... Sept. 13
12:12 .... June 22
13:8 .... Nov. 20
13:11 .... Jan. 19
14:22 .... Nov. 22
15:7 .... Apr. 3
15:22 .... Jan. 7
16:2 .... May 31
16:20 .... July 6

I CORINTHIANS

1:4 .... Oct. 8
1:8 .... Aug. 29
3:4 .... May 29
4:17, 20 .... Sept. 3
5:6 .... Aug. 13
6:12 .... Aug. 12
7:15 .... Aug. 14

8:1, 3 .... July 24
9:24 .... Jan. 24
10:13 .... Oct. 13
10:13 .... Oct. 27
11:17, 18 .... July 26
12:18 .... July 2
13:4 .... Feb. 14
14:3 .... July 1
15:10 .... June 30
15:42 .... Apr. 9
16:14 .... Apr. 10

2 CORINTHIANS

1:10, 11 .... Dec. 22
1:22 .... Dec. 15
4:18 .... Jan. 4
5:6 .... Mar. 25
6:1 .... Apr. 11
6:2 .... Mar. 3
6:13 .... Oct. 4
7:1 .... Mar. 24
8:5 .... May 30
10:6 .... Oct. 6
11:15 .... Aug. 6

GALATIANS

1:24 .... Nov. 26
3:9 .... Oct. 5
5:6 .... May 5

COLOSSIANS

1:11 .... Feb. 10
3:15 .... Sept. 14

1 THESSALONIANS

1:3 .... Mar. 5
1:9 .... Feb. 24
2:4 .... July 7
3:12 .... July 9
5:8 .... Mar. 12
5:9 .... July 10

2 THESSALONIANS

1:3 .... July 11
1:3 .... Sept. 16
1:11 .... Feb. 23
2:14 .... July 12
2:15 .... Mar. 13

1 TIMOTHY

1:5, 6 .... July 14
1:15 .... Sept. 9
2:2 .... July 15
2:9 .... Mar. 2
4:4 .... Jan. 8
4:16 .... Sept. 17
6:1 .... July 5
6:18, 19 .... Mar. 1

Scriptural Index

2 TIMOTHY

1:7 .... Feb. 28
2:15 .... Mar. 15
3:1 .... Apr. 5

TITUS

2:1 .... July 16

PHILEMON

7 .... July 19

HEBREWS

2:1 .... Mar. 19
3:6 .... July 21
4:7 .... Oct. 12
5:2 .... July 18

6:13 .... July 17
10:24 .... Mar. 17
10:39 .... Mar. 16
12:1 .... Dec. 4
13:5, 6 .... Dec. 19
13:15, 16 .... Apr. 19
13:21 .... Oct. 22

JAMES

1:12 .... Apr. 30
1:19 .... May 18
1:25 .... Apr. 21
1:25 .... Dec. 21
3:1 .... Dec. 27
4:2, 3 .... Jan. 26
4:8 .... Dec. 5
4:17 .... Sept. 7
5:5 .... Dec. 12
5:11 .... Dec. 2
5:16 .... Dec. 3

1 PETER

1:4 .... Nov. 15
1:8 .... July 25
2:12 .... Dec. 13
4:10, 11 .... Sept. 25

1 JOHN

1:7 .... Aug. 31
3:21 .... Dec. 26
5:3 .... Aug. 27
5:10 .... Nov. 6

REVELATION

3:1 .... Dec. 16
3:8, 12 .... Sept. 27
5:8 .... May 11
7:17 .... May 12
12:9 .... Apr. 6
12:11 .... Apr. 6
20:13 .... May 7
22:9 .... Jan. 5